HISPANIC
NOTES & MONOGRAPHS

ESSAYS, STUDIES, AND BRIEF
BIOGRAPHIES ISSUED BY THE
HISPANIC SOCIETY OF AMERICA

VII

SOME MASTERS
OF
SPANISH VERSE

BY

JAMES FITZMAURICE-KELLY, F.B.A.

Essay Index Reprint Series

Originally published by:
OXFORD UNIVERSITY PRESS

BOOKS FOR LIBRARIES PRESS, INC.
FREEPORT, NEW YORK

First published 1924
Reprinted 1967

Reprinted from a copy in the collections of
The New York Public Library
Astor, Lenox and Tilden Foundations

PRINTED IN THE UNITED STATES OF AMERICA

PREFACE

SOME years ago the Special Board of Modern Languages at Cambridge did me the honour to invite me to address them on a subject of Spanish literature. They left me complete freedom as to the choice of a theme. There were no exclusions, but this does not mean that there were no preferences. It was suggested to me that *The Oxford Book of Spanish Verse* would be acceptable. Apart from any other recommendation, the plan proposed had the advantage of enabling me to concentrate on a single genre. This volume embodies the result of the suggestion, with some additions and with the omission of the lectures dealing respectively with the *romanceros* and with *Luis de Leon* (who has already formed the subject of a monograph in this series).

J. F.-K.

WALBERSWICK. August 1923.

CONTENTS

		PAGE
	PREFACE	v
I.	BERCEO AND OTHER FORE-RUNNERS	1
II.	GARCI LASSO DE LA VEGA	43
III.	TWO MYSTIC POETS	73
IV.	LOPE DE VEGA	94
V.	LUIS DE GÓNGORA	119
VI.	SOME LATER POETS	153
	NOTES	183
	INDEX	184

BERCEO, ETC.

BERCEO AND OTHER FORERUNNERS

IN the subsequent chapters we are concerned, not with old Spanish epical verse and the intricate problems it presents, but with the main body of Spanish poetry, beginning at the outset. Spanish literature has qualities of its own: a poignant, merciless realism, mingled with a mystic *abandon*, which makes a stirring appeal to a certain type of reader. This reader has something to put up with. The Spanish language is not particularly ductile: there are tongues more subtle, more malleable, more perfectly adequate as instruments of delicate expression. Still, Spanish combines, in an unsurpassed degree, verbal melody with martial clangour, and its wealth of diminutives adds to its resources notes of caressing tenderness. The very sounds of certain Spanish words thrill some of us with an exquisite delight, and may even tend to obscure our critical judgement: it is, perhaps, not easy to rid oneself of all bias in favour of a man with a name so charming as Mira de Mescua. Nevertheless, it would be misleading to convey the impression that the best Spanish verse has all the magic lyrical quality of the greatest English verse. It is more facile and less inevitable; its beauty is less inherent, less haunting. And, as it has no tradition so splendid and so unbroken, it has less of the charm of association. Spanish verse was slower in sloughing off its derivative character; its period of magnificence was of shorter duration; its eclipse came suddenly, its soul was required of it in the night. Withal, it has, I repeat, arresting traits. These revealed themselves with some deliberation, and, as I propose to follow as closely as may be the chronological order of production, there is a chance that at the outset the reader may be led

FORERUNNERS

to accept George Borrow's hasty conclusion that the literature of Spain is not altogether worthy of the language. Should he take that view, it will be comprehensible, and even excusable. None the less, he will be mistaken, even as Borrow was mistaken. He will have lost sight of the essential fact that the ideals of art vary in varying latitudes. In the north, the artist's chief care is for perfection of detail; his compeer, south of the Pyrenees, is mainly concerned with breadth of massive effect.

Apparently the earliest Spanish poet whose name drifts down to us is Gonzalo de Berceo. Not, of course, that Berceo, as we call him, is a genuine surname (in Spain as elsewhere, authentic surnames belong to a much later period). Berceo is in reality a place-name, the name of a village in the district of Rioja near Nájera. Nájera is not unfamiliar to students of English or Spanish history: there the Black Prince won a victory in the spring of 1367, and there he took prisoner the Chancellor of Castile, Pero Lopez de Ayala, famous as a statesman, a courtier, a poet, and a chronicler. But we must not anticipate events. Gonzalo flourished about a century and a half earlier than Lopez de Ayala, was brought up in Berceo as a boy, took orders, and was finally attached as a secular priest to the neighbouring monastery of San Millan de la Cogolla (Modern Spanish *cogulla* = a cowl, from the Latin *cuculla*). That is practically all we know in the way of personal details about Berceo; for the date of his birth is not recorded, and the date of his death is uncertain. He is last heard of in 1246 when he signed a legal document as witness, and it seems probable that he did not live long afterwards.

From the Benedictines at San Millan de la Cogolla in the diocese of Calahorra in the province of Old Castile, Berceo learned nearly all he knew. At San Millan de la Cogolla his natural taste for devout legends and pietistic traditions was developed, and in the fullness of time he began to write in imitation of the monks among whom he moved. The north of Spain had in his time successfully beaten off the Arab onset. The Benedictines from the mother-house at Cluny were the centre of intellectual life in Spain. Laymen were too busily engaged in fighting to have time for culture. Poetry fell into the hands of clerics and of popular singers, wandering minstrels whose untutored measures were called the *mester de joglaría*. The better educated, or more pretentious, poets wrote in the *cuaderna vía*: monorhymed Alexandrine quatrains, a metrical design frequent in pious compositions, and often called, from its most assiduous practitioners, the clerkly measure or *mester de clerecía*. As became a disciple of the Benedictines, Berceo wrote mostly in this comparatively learned metre; his subjects, as might be expected, are always devotional in character; but he never drew aloof from the people. Even in the midst of his pious recitals, he will introduce a trait of quiet, unsmiling humour, and his patriotism is manifested in his unconcealed preference for Spanish saints: not only San Millan, a local celebrity whom he was officially bound to praise, but St. Lawrence, a native of Huesca, and Santo Domingo de Silos, who founded near Burgos the celebrated Benedictine monastery of San Sebastian de Silos, a famous centre of Spanish learning during the Middle Ages.

Berceo, then, dwelt among his own people, sharing their tastes, sympathies, preferences, and prejudices. He was not a great poet, and could never, in the most favourable circumstances, have become one. He is imitative, and piques himself on his close adherence to his originals. 'We set down that only which we read', he says with a certain touch of proud humility.

Al non escribimos si non lo que leemos.

Berceo declares that he is not learned enough to write in Latin: he must perforce content himself with the *romanz paladino* — the vernacular in which, as he says, honest, plain people talk to one another. Berceo's use of the vernacular reveals his popular sympathies; he is obviously interested in the poetry of the *juglares* (or *jongleurs*) who spoke for the multitude, and, in the middle of his pietistic narratives, he does not hesitate to reproduce as closely as possible the current epical formulae. Had Berceo not been saturated in Spanish epical poetry he would never have described San Millan as *el buen campeador*, or Garcia as a *noble campeador*, or Santo Domingo as one *que nasció en buen punto*. These phrases, and many others like unto them, are unmistakable reminiscences of the *Poema del Cid*, and though, for form's sake, Berceo may protest now and then that his *prosas* and *dictados* are not to be confounded with the *cantares* of the more popular *juglares*, this is only a *façon de parler*, a saving assertion of professional dignity. When he is off his guard, the truth escapes him; he calls himself the *juglar* of Santo

Domingo de Silos, and he appeals for largesse in the spirit, and almost in the very words, of the *juglar* of the *Poema del Cid*, suggesting that a glass of good wine would be particularly acceptable.

Bien valdrá, como creo, un vaso de bon vino.

It is precisely this popular savour which keeps Berceo alive for us. In telling us of the miracles of his canonized saints and devout heroes, he incidentally portrays the material existence of the farmers, the monks, the lower middle-classes of Old Castile. It is part of his enduring charm that Berceo remains a simple village priest, sharing the views of his simple-hearted flock, and retaining something of the Spanish peasant's reticent joviality. He has also the verbal fluency of the Castilian peasant, and his copiousness runs to about 13,000 lines in the works which are indisputably his. It has further been sought to magnify his achievement by ascribing to him the *Libro de Alexandre,* and his name is attached to this composition in one extant manuscript. We need not accept this attribution as an article of faith. The text of the *Libro de Alexandre* is honeycombed with Leonese words and forms; these are so numerous that they cannot well be entirely imputed to the scribe or copyist, and these traces of Leonese cannot possibly be due to Berceo himself. The content of the *Libro de Alexandre* points to the same conclusion. It is essentially a learned poem written by somebody who had read Gautier de Châtillon, the Pseudo-Callisthenes, Josephus, Statius, *Floire et Blanceflor*, the work of Lambert le Tors, and many other compilations of the same kind. This erudition is quite beyond Berceo. By no stretching of language can he be called learned, and he had no marked taste for the allegory which is so prominent in the *Libro de Alexandre*. The writer of the *Libro de Alexandre* is a bit of an historian, an astronomer, and even a geologist. He is a didactic moralist with a much greater insight into the ways of the world than is to be observed in Berceo's authentic works. He has not Berceo's purity of diction, nor is his syntax enriched by the same familiarity with popular constructions and idiomatic phrases. We cannot tell what evidence may be discovered in the future, but the facts before us should make us hesitate to accept the ascription of the *Libro de Alexandre* to Berceo. This theory has not even in its favour the attraction of novelty: it was first put forward over a century ago by Rafael Floranes, and during more than a hundred years it has not made a single convert of importance.

Berceo would have been surprised to know that he was supposed to have written a production so learned. He himself valued most highly his life of Santa Oria; but his taste was not infallible, and the judgement of authors on their works is not to be blindly followed. As the *Vida de Santa Oria, Virgen* was, as Berceo tells us, the child of his old age, we perhaps ought to make some deduction for parental

FORERUNNERS

partiality. To many of us more attraction is found in the naïf *Milagros de Nuestra Señora*, which he appears to have drawn from mediaeval Latin sources. Still, it is in the Lament of our Lady—in the *Duelo que fizo la Virgen Maria*—that he is most lyrical. He seems to break away from his usual *prosas*, and at the very end he departs wholly from the monotonous *mester de clerecía*. In the song which has for a refrain the words '*Eya velar*', Berceo experiments in a new metre. Tomas Antonio Sanchez, Berceo's first editor, was no doubt right in regarding this composition as a sort of litany, a kind of *villancico* with a burden. The presence of the refrain *Eya velar* would naturally lead us to suspect that the verses were intended to be chanted. The lines themselves are 'singable' (if there be such a word) and, to place the matter beyond doubt, the heading in the codex is *Cantica*. It is customary to print these verses as though they were Alexandrines; but a very superficial examination will show that the song is written in rhymed pairs of lines—such as are found in other, probably older, forms of Spanish verse (in *Santa Maria Egipciaca*, for instance). This song is supposed to be sung by the Jews who were guarding the Saviour's sepulchre. As has been said before, this *estribillo* or refrain—*eya velar*—is an almost certain indication that the verses were intended to be sung—most likely in the open air—and, in the opinion of that very learned lady, Doña Carolina Michaëlis de Vasconcellos, it is in a very high degree probable that the idea of this singular composition was suggested to Berceo by some of the *muiñeiras* which he might easily have heard intoned by Portuguese pilgrims on their way to Santiago de Compostela. The conjecture is ingenious and plausible. Such spontaneous song would appeal to Berceo's simple-hearted piety and inherent liking for popular forms of art. Bouterwek, writing over a century ago, expressed the view that Spaniards were prone to exaggerate

Berceo's merits. This is hard to believe, as the first complete edition of Berceo was not printed till near the end of the eighteenth century, so that when Bouterwek wrote, very few Spaniards, outside a small circle of scholars, had ever heard his name. The situation has changed since, and few competent judges would venture to dissent from the opinion of Menéndez y Pelayo that Berceo's simple numbers have more charm than most of the alembicated poems in the fifteenth-century *Cancioneros*. He has his defects, of course. By some negligence he allows the Jews to speak of Christ as the Son of God; his versification lacks finish; but his diction is technically correct, and the few remarks to be made upon it are rather explanatory than critical. Berceo, I may remark, has not been well treated by translators, for though there are fragmentary renderings of him by John Hookham Frere and Longfellow, neither has chosen a passage interesting in itself, or specially characteristic of the author.

Alfonso X need not detain us as a Castilian poet, although, if he wrote all the Galician poems ascribed to him, he must have had extraordinary fluency. With the exception of the fragment

> *Senhora, por amor de Dios*
> *aued alguno duelo de my,*

his Castilian verses have not survived, and these few lines càme down to us highly Galicianized. So careful as he was in organizing learning, Alfonso X was a most incompetent ruler, and his incompetency bore fruit in abundance. His reign closed in the horrors of a civil war; his son Sancho IV, a usurper if there ever was one, was perpetually engaged in battles with his brothers, and the recalcitrant nobles and prelates who supported them. Sancho's son, Fernando IV, was an infant when he came to the throne, and died at the age of seventeen. Then followed another minority—that of Alfonso XI—and anarchy was rampant everywhere. In such circumstances we cannot afford to be too severe in judging Juan Ruiz who wrote in the fourteenth century. As in the case of Berceo we know next to nothing about the man. He hints that he was born at Alcalá de Henares; the date of his birth is conjecturally fixed at about 1283; he became archpriest of Fita (now Hita); he was sent to prison by Cardinal Gil de Albornoz, a very respectable ecclesiastic; and the copyist of one of the manuscripts of his poems states that Juan Ruiz wrote his verses while in jail. That is all that we know about Juan Ruiz; but a good deal more may be inferred from his *Libro de buen amor*— a strange medley of truth, fiction, devout moods, picaresque wit, and unedifying revelations. We cannot feel sure that his imprisonment was quite so unjust as he declared it to be. There is a tendency nowadays to accept this assertion as conclusive, but one scarcely sees why, except in the interest of a deliberate policy of whitewashing. That policy has long been pursued, and has not hitherto been effective. When I read that Ruiz voluntarily became a 'holocaust of the moral idea which he championed', I am not nearly so sure as I should like to be that I understand the meaning of the phrase. 'Moral ideas' do not greatly abound in Juan Ruiz, who seems to have been an incorrigibly criminous clerk. If one denies that, so it seems to me, one closes one's eyes to the facts, and to the sly humour of his contrasts between the *loco amor* (worldly love) and the *buen amor* (divine love). Ruiz evidently knows a great deal more about the former than about the latter, and his knowledge is evidently at first hand

Ruiz, like Berceo, was a village priest, and he has left us a description of his personal appearance, less attractive, but perhaps even more convincing than Cervantes's famous portrait of himself. The Archpriest, as he informs us, was more than common tall, was sturdy, thick-set, hairy, full-chested, bull-necked, black-eyed, with thick eyebrows, neat legs, small feet, sensuous lips, large ears, and expansive nostrils. This is not the portrait of an ascetic, and the Archpriest was assuredly nothing of the kind. Had he been an ascetic, he would not, could not, have written the *Libro de buen amor*. Compared with Berceo, Juan Ruiz might be called learned: not that he was an exact scholar: rather, a desultory, omnivorous reader, with an infinite gusto for literature. He borrows freely in all directions. He takes from *Pamphilus de Amore*, and transforms its licentious tedium into vivid reality; he rifles the oriental apologues and charges every rift with his own precious ore; with incomparable dexterity, he transplants to Spanish soil what best suits his purpose in French literature—some form of what he calls 'Ysopete', a handful of *contes*, a clutch of *pastourelles*, a selection of *fabliaux*, an adaptation of the *Bataille de Karesme et de Charnage*. All these themes are enriched in their passage into Spanish: Ruiz handles them all with a liberty of expression and an intelligent freedom of thought which have led some to regard him as a sort of religious reformer. He was nothing of the kind. He was the incarnation of his own loose age, observant of religious formulae, but not inspired by any breath of devotional fervour. He is all of this world, mundane, with a keen eye for the picaresque side of life. He abounds in satirical observation, but is never indignant after the fashion of the scandalized moralist. He is too much concerned with the panorama of existence to spare a word of censure. He is too intent on seeing to have time for evangelizing. And he sees with such picturesque penetration and renders with such graphic fidelity that his principal types re-appear again and again in later literature. His Don Furon meets us again in *Lazarillo de Tormes*, and perhaps in *Pickwick*; Trotaconventos comes to life once more in Régnier's Macette as well as in the *Celestina*, and who can feel sure that she has not counted for something in the conception of Juliet's nurse?

FORERUNNERS

Withal, the Archpriest's originality lies greatly in his style—succulent, careless, but racy of the soil. He prided himself on his versification. He has done wonders in breaking down the stiff formation of the *mester de clerecía*, in experimenting in new metres. Without any hesitation he avows that he has left no kind unattempted, that he has written dance-songs and serenades innumerable for Moorish and Jewish dancing-girls, for blind men, for nocturnal wandering students. 'As to my *cantares cazurros*,' he says later, 'ten MS. books would not contain them.' One specimen has survived in the *trova cazurra* beginning

> *Mys ojos non verán luz*
> *pues perdido he a cruz.*

'My eyes will see no light,' says this incredible Archpriest, 'for I have lost Cruz.' Cruz or Cross would appear to be the lady's name, either her real name or one given her by the poet, who seems to have suffered at her hands. We are left to surmise that the lady was of short stature, since the Archpriest tells us of his distaste for the opposite type in a rhymed summary, of which Longfellow has made a translation: a translation not generally known, as it is hidden in the *North American Review* for April 1833. (1)

I wish to make my sermon brief, to shorten my oration,
For a never-ending sermon is my utter detestation,
I like short women,— suits-at-law without procrastination,
And am always most delighted with things of short duration.

A babbler is a laughing-stock, he's a fool who's always grinning,
But little women love so much, one falls in love with sinning.
There are women who are very tall, and yet not worth the winning,
And in the change of short for long repentance finds beginning.

To praise the little women, Love besought me in my musing,
To tell their noble qualities is quite beyond refusing,

So I'll praise the little women, and you'll
 find the thing amusing;
They are I know as cold as snow, whilst
 flames around diffusing.

They're cold without, whilst warm within
 the flame of Love is raging,
They're gay and pleasant in the street,—soft,
 cheerful and engaging,
They're thrifty and discreet at home,—the
 cares of life assuaging,
All this and more—try, and you'll find how
 true is my presaging.

In a little precious stone, what splendour
 meets the eyes!
In a little lump of sugar how much of sweet-
 ness lies!
So in a little woman love grows and
 multiplies,
You recollect the proverb says—a word unto
 the wise.

A peppercorn is very small, but seasons
 every dinner
More than all other condiments, although
 'tis sprinkled thinner,

Just so a little woman is, if Love will let you win her,
There's not a joy in all the world you will not find within her.

And as within the little rose you find the richest dyes,
And in a little grain of gold much price and value lies,
As from a little balsam much odor doth arise,
So in a little woman there's a taste of paradise!

Even as the little ruby its secret worth betrays,
Color and price and virtue, in the clearness of its rays,—
Just so a little woman much excellence displays,
Beauty and grace and love and fidelity always.

The sky-lark and the nightingale, though small and light of wing,
Yet warble sweeter in the grove than all the birds that sing,

And so a little woman, though a very little
 thing,
Is sweeter far than sugar, and flowers that
 bloom in spring.

The magpie and the golden thrush have
 many a thrilling note,
Each as a gay musician doth strain his little
 throat,
A merry little songster in his green and
 yellow coat,
And such a little woman is when love doth
 make her doat.

There's nought can be compared to her,
 throughout the wide creation,
She is a paradise on earth,—our greatest
 consolation,—
So cheerful, gay and happy, so free from
 all vexation,
In fine, she's better in the proof than in
 anticipation.

If as her size increases are woman's charms
 decreased,
Then surely it is good to be from all the
 great released,

> Now of two evils choose the less,—said a
>   wise man of the East,
> By consequence, of woman-kind be sure to
>   choose the least.

This represents the Archpriest in a characteristically reckless mood, a master of his instrument even when he has little to say. He lives by virtue of these qualities —force, power of creation, knowledge of life, metrical resource—all of which combine to make him the most eminent figure and most imposing personality of early Spanish literature.

The next name on our list is that of Pero Lopez de Ayala (1333-1407), a Basque who, like most of his contemporaries, knew how to feather his nest well. He soon obtained a post at court and stood by Peter till 1366, when the Pretender, Henry of Trastamara, was proclaimed king at Calahorra. This looked serious, and Lopez de Ayala (and his father) thought it high time to go over to the other—the bastard's—side. He records this defection with amazing coolness, not to say impudence. 'And King Peter's affairs were now in such a state that those who left him made up their minds not to come back.' This remark is Spanish in its candour and is highly characteristic of the man. Lopez de Ayala served his employers well, but he had no liking for being on the losing side, and he had a keen eye for the main chance. His calculations were not always right. He was captured by the Black Prince at Nájera (1367) and was again taken prisoner when John I was defeated by the Portuguese at Aljubarrota (1385). But he knew how to turn even his misfortunes to good account. The Portuguese shut him up in an iron cage at Oviedes. He had in hand at the time a long poem entitled *Rimado de Palacio*, and he philosophically settled down to continue this in his cage. It has been said that part of the *Rimado* was written in England, but there is no proof that Lopez de Ayala ever visited this country.

The *Rimado de Palacio* is not a collection of courtly verses : it is rather a general satire on society. And though Lopez de Ayala has not the Archpriest's knowledge of the lower classes, his satire in the first part of his poem is as wide in range, and more merciless in spirit. Every one comes under his lash, from popes downwards. While he is in this vein of universal denunciation, Lopez de Ayala is at his best : later in the poem he subsides into a gentler, more edifying, but less interesting mood. In form, speaking generally, he belongs to the old school and usually adheres to the *cuaderna vía* : but not always ; he has reminiscences of Galician writers and even attempts the verses of *arte mayor*; but he was too old to learn new tricks, and finally returns to the *cuaderna vía* again.

As a prose-writer he excels. His treatises on falconry, the translations of Livy, St. Isidore, St. Gregory, Boccaccio, and the like, are eclipsed by his chronicles of the reigns of Peter the Cruel, Henry II, John I, and Henry III (he died as he reached the end of 1396, so his account of Henry III was left incomplete). He is not a great historical artist, but he had a first-hand knowledge of the matter which he communicated ; he has a considerable, and even disconcerting, gift of neutrality, and if he is not interested in movements, he has a rare power of portraying individuals. He is 'suspect' in the case of Peter the Cruel, but otherwise his impartiality is extraordinary. His translation of a Latin treatise by Boccaccio deserves special mention, for it indicates the dawn of the Italian influence in Spain, an influence to which we shall often have to recur later.

Ayala died in 1407. A year before that date we come to the Infant-King of Spain, John II : an exceedingly inefficient monarch, but a patron of letters in an amateurish, dilettante way. During the many hours which John II devoted to the neglect of his duties, he versified himself, and, encouraging others to versify, made his court into a little nest of singing-birds whose notes, if neither sweet nor strong, were persistent and all-pervading. It would be a gross exaggeration to say that John II brought poetry into fashion: poetry, thank Heaven, springs immortal. But John II's ostentatious leaning to versification made it easier for a gentleman to write verse without any fear of being thought finicky or effeminate. The King thus transferred the practice of verse-making from humble *juglares* and dusty monks to gleaming nobles and shining knights: unconsciously and even unintentionally, he was beginning the tradition of a learned, or at least an accomplished, aristocracy in Spain. What knights and nobles could do without reproach could be done later by the middle classes without fear of losing caste. And this is precisely what happened.

John II was not alone in countenancing literature. A kinsman of his, Enrique de Villena, often wrongly called the Marqués de Villena, was no less zealous in the good cause. Villena (for a man in his position) was learned and diligent; but though he set a good example of industry, it must be frankly said that he had little or no literary gifts. Still, he did something to promote an interest in literature, and for this he deserves thanks and some honour. He seems to have dabbled in metrics and to have written verses; if so, they have not survived. We have various miscellanies of his, but they might as well have disappeared too, for nobody reads them. Villena's best work (and I hasten to say that it is not good) was done as a translator. He did Virgil and Dante into Spanish prose, and thus brought two great masters within reach of everybody in Spain. The translation of Dante, poor as it is, serves to denote an increased interest in Italian literature, the dawn of which we saw in Lopez de Ayala with his translation of Boccaccio. But when all is said and done, it cannot be denied that the power of Villena lies rather in his personality—his legend, if you prefer to say that—than in his work. His prose is as bad as bad can be. I hesitate to call him the worst prose-writer in the whole history of Spanish literature; but I can think of nobody who is below him. On the other hand, the man's personality has colour and picturesqueness; his knowledge of languages—which included Arabic, Hebrew, and (it is said) even a little Greek—was looked upon as miraculous, not to say uncanny. It was noised about that he was an enchanter; part of his library, supposed to be contaminated as a source of its owner's mastery of the black arts, was burned after his death; and his fame as a wizard lasted long after him and afforded a subject of treatment to writers so diverse in time and temper as Quevedo and Hartzenbusch, not to mention the two seventeenth-century dramatists, Ruiz de Alarcon and Rojas Zorrilla.

For John II's reign the *corpus poeticum* is a collection of verses known as the *Cancionero de Baena*, Juan Alfonso Baena being the name of the editor or anthologist.

Baena, who has often been described (without any good reason) as a Jew, was no genius; he lacked art and he lacked taste, as he showed by omitting from his anthology the only really good poem that he ever wrote. His merits are that he is a representative of the Galician school of verse, and that in his collection, made about 1445, which exemplifies the junction of the Galician and Castilian, we are furnished with interesting specimens of verses which would otherwise be unknown to us, and which have a pristine value. Baena's collection covers a long period and includes the work of some poets who were dead. As regards the living, many omissions are noticeable. Perhaps the earliest poet included by Baena is the Archdeacon of Toro, whose name was Gonçalo Rodriguez, as my friend, Mr. Aubrey Bell, has pointed out. He has touches of pagan levity which suggest a remote kinship with Browning's bishop who ordered his tomb in St. Praxed's church; but besides his *insouciant* humour he deserves recognition for the technical skill which entitles him to rank as a representative of the Galician school. Another Galician no less skilful in the management of metres was Alfonso Alvarez de Villasandino, often a poet and almost invariably a sturdy, shameless beggar. Two other Galicians deserve mention in connexion with this *Cancionero* : a certain Macias, *o Namorado*, and Juan Rodriguez de la Cámara (o del Padron, from his birthplace). It is alleged that Macias was in the household of Villena, but as Villena was not born till 1384 and as Macias appears to have died in 1390, this seems unlikely. There is really very little to say about the enamoured Macias as a poet, for his name is attached to only five copies of mediocre verses in the *Cancionero*. Like Villena, he is more interesting as a traditional figure than as an executant artist. A current story is that owing to some obscure love-affair he was imprisoned in Arjonilla; another version runs that the jealous husband of his lady overheard

FORERUNNERS

him singing his love-plaint: whereon the husband flung a javelin through the open window and thus slew the enamoured one. The truth of this legend, and of other legends like unto it, is very contestable: it seems quite possible that a myth may have been evolved from Macias's poem: *Ai sennora, en quen fiança.* However it grew into existence, it became wonderfully popular and has been treated by poets like Santillana, by great prose-writers like the author of the *Celestina* and (twice) by Mariano José de Larra, best known by his pseudonym of *Fígaro*. A very similar legend has gathered round Macias's admirer, Juan Rodriguez de la Cámara, who is supposed to have died about the middle of the fifteenth century. He is said to have had at least two queens in love with him: Isabel, who was afterwards the second wife of John II, a Portuguese princess whom there is no reason to suppose that he ever saw; Juana, who married Henry IV in 1455, when Rodriguez was dead. The foundation for these stories is, apparently, that he had some exciting love-passages with a court-lady, with such poor results that he went out of his mind. Rodriguez de la Cámara deserves a place in the history of literature as a novelist of a sentimental style. His authentic poems alone would scarcely entitle him to figure there : these mediocre poems—about twenty in number—are scattered about his novel—*El siervo libre de Amor*—and in certain collections of verse. There is for example in the British Museum a manuscript wherein Rodriguez de la Cámara's name is attached to three celebrated *romances—Conde Arnaldos, Rosa florida,* and *La Infantina.* If this ascription is correct, we should have to reconsider our estimate of Rodriguez de la Cámara as a poet, for they are much above his usual level. He only contributed one poem to the *Cancionero de Baena,* and this is not great poetry : far from it. It has, however, one feature that distinguishes it. It is written in Castilian, and, as Rodriguez de la Cámara was

FORERUNNERS

a Galician, this circumstance is worth noting: for it clearly indicates that Castilian was attaining a linguistic hegemony.

Another influence is noticeable in the *Cancionero de Baena*: an increase of the Italian element foreshadowed, as we have seen, by the efforts of Lopez de Ayala and Villena. The man in whom this tendency was more marked still was Francisco Imperial who appears to have been the son of an Italian settled in Seville. The *Dezir a las syete virtudes*, in the *Cancionero de Baena*, is really a *pastiche* of various passages in Dante's *Divina Commedia*. It is not great poetry for the simple reason that it is not original, being, in fact, sometimes a rather pallid versified version of Dante's austere Muse. But it emphasizes a new tendency in Spanish versification which was to become more and more marked as time went on. Though anything but a genius, Imperial did something great in imparting to Spanish literature a direction from which it never swerved

AND MONOGRAPHS

later. Imperial appears to have made an immediate impression, for echoes of Italian influence are obvious on contemporaries like Gonzalo Martinez de Medina who talks glibly of Guelphs and Ghibellines and appears to have known Boccaccio. Probably another contemporary who also contributed to the *Cancionero de Baena*—I mean Ruy Paez de Ribera— was likewise influenced by Imperial's example. He has a stray note of realism, and expresses with poignant vigour the misery of poverty and the infirmities of age.

There is, too, a considerable dose of Italianism in the form of the celebrated Iñigo Lopez de Mendoza whom it is convenient to call by one of his titles, the Marqués de Santillana (his other title is the Conde del Real de Manzanares, but that is not so comfortably short). Santillana had an hereditary interest in poetry, for he was the son of that Diego Hurtado de Mendoza whose delightful *cossante* begins *A aquel arbol, que mueve la foxa.* At a very early age Santillana (who did not receive his titles, I may remark, till after the battle of Olmedo in 1445) manifested his literary inclinations, and made friends with Villena, who dedicated to him his versions of Virgil and Dante. At this time Santillana was but a boy, but he was already a person of note. He played a prominent part in the political struggles of his time, changing sides opportunely, being now for, and now against John II as his interests directed. This does not make him a sympathetic figure to posterity, but his political variability is forgotten while his literature survives. There is Italianism in Santillana, no doubt; but we need not exaggerate it. It is not very emphatic in *La Comedieta de Ponça*, though Boccaccio is introduced into this poem and even speaks in Italian, and the general idea owes something to Petrarch. It is more pronounced in an earlier composition, the *Triunphete de Amor*, which is manifestly inspired by Petrarch's *Triunfi*. Again the influence of Dante is obvious in *El infierno de los enamorados*. Santillana would doubtless have gloried in being thought a follower of the Italians, for he took a great pride in his forty-two sonnets, *fechos al itálico modo*, as he is careful to say. But he assimilated Italian literature as he assimilated the literature of other countries. Though not learned, he was accomplished and many-sided. He took what he could from Latin, read Greek authors in Latin versions, was an assiduous follower of French poets, some of whom—Jean de Meung, Othon de Granson, and Alain Chartier—he mentions by name in a famous letter to the Constable of Portugal, written probably not later than 1449. But, after all, Santillana does not live by his learned poems, but by his gay songs—*dezires*, *serranillas*, and *vaqueiras*—compositions redolent of the soil, graceful, seductive in their ingenuous spontaneity and simplicity. In these lyrical bursts, he harmonizes the cruder realism of Ruiz and, if not uninfluenced by foreign models, his art reflects the charm of his engaging personality.

Santillana seems to have been the friend and perhaps even the patron of a younger contemporary poet, Juan de Mena (1411–56), whom he outlived by a couple of years. It is a little difficult to do full justice to Mena, who has created a prejudice against himself by his detestable prose, which is perhaps as bad as that of Villena. This is saying a great deal, but it can be maintained. He had the bad luck to go to Italy in his youth, was there attacked by a craze for latinizing his own language and was led into all manner of obscurities, some of which disfigure his verse as well as his prose. But in his verse these defects are less noticeable, and, after all, it is by his verse that Mena must be judged. Not all of this survives, but *El Laberinto de Fortuna* still finds readers and exhibits him at his best. In this allegory, as elsewhere, he is embarrassed by inopportune learning, as one might guess from the title alone.

This title was for a long while displaced by another unauthorized one—*Las Trezientas*—which became current. One legend is that Mena added a total of three stanzas to the original 297 to make his poem correspond to the title commonly given to it and that John II, with whom the poem was a favourite, asked Mena to write sixty-five supplementary stanzas so that there might be a stanza for each day of the year. This would appear to be an idle invention. It is a fact that twenty-seven supplementary octaves were written, but they can scarcely be by Mena who, as a royal chronicler, was almost bound to be considerate to his employer, while the supplementary verses reflect rather severely on John II's character and conduct.

There are traits of pedantry in *El Laberinto*, and the general effect of allegory is apt to be tiresome nowadays to ordinary readers, who weary not a little of the reminiscences of Latin poets and the recurrence of visions after Dante, a very long way after Dante. But this is hardly fair to Mena who has distinct poetic gifts of his own: an ardent vision of the past, a keen sense of the significance of historical events, and a magnificent rhetoric always sincere, and sometimes touched with imaginative splendour. There are flat passages in *El Laberinto*, but there is a compensating quality in many of Mena's octaves joined to a dignified patriotism which appeals more or less strongly to all his countrymen even to this day. Mena will never be popular: it can scarcely be supposed that he expected to be, otherwise he would hardly have cultivated so assiduously the obscurities which must always alienate readers from him. But the fact remains that as a writer of *versos de arte mayor* he has no superior and scarcely any equal, and this technical excellence endured a vogue which lasted at least a hundred years. It is remarkable that Cervantes and Lope de Vega, who so seldom were of the same mind on literary subjects, joined in praising him, and foreigners, who do not share their view, may perhaps be expected to receive it with respect, if not docility. Mena lost himself in a jungle of false principles: the idea of re-latinizing Castilian was doomed to failure in advance. But he could not foresee this, and it is fair to add that a great many words introduced by him, which raised a storm at the time, have now been received into the substance of the language and are used daily without exciting objection or even raising a remark.

GARCI LASSO DE LA VEGA

It is perhaps not altogether fanciful to regard, in one's mind's eye, the three chief literatures of Western Europe as though they were so many landscapes, alike in some minor details, but with marked differences of contour. Spanish and English literature are (so to say) based on a fairly high tableland, from which gigantic peaks tower up suddenly: such peaks as Shakespeare, and Lope de Vega, and Cervantes, and Milton, and Calderon. French literature is based on a higher tableland, but the peaks which detach themselves (if one may say so, without any disrespect to Molière and Corneille and Racine) are perhaps less numerous and are certainly less imposing. Still, up to the present stage of our examination of Spanish verse, it must be admitted that, with the single and signal exception of the Archpriest of Hita, we have not met with any dominating personality. Individual Spaniards are nearly always precocious, but the literature of Spain was slow in coming to maturity. Great personalities are wont to appear in great periods, and the great period of Spanish history can scarcely be said to begin much before the end of the fifteenth century. The air of Spain echoed with twitterings and pipings from the court-poets who thronged round John II, himself an incorrigible poetaster in the long spells of time which he devoted to indolent frivolities. He and those about him had little to say (that was worth saying) in verse; the forms in which they wrote were exhausted, as it seemed, and appeared inadequate to the noble expression of sublime and subtle thoughts. Not that we need suppose that such thoughts obsessed John II and his compeers who were quite content to carve cherry-stones. The turbulent reign of Henry IV was obviously not propitious to literature. The reign of the Catholic Kings, Ferdinand and Isabel, was incontestably a great period; but all the available energies of their subjects were absorbed in the solution of practical problems, and in the re-establishment of peace at home, if not abroad. The work of pacification was at last accomplished. Before Charles V came to the throne, circumstances had combined to enforce the general recognition of Spain's practical achievement. It remained for her to prove what she could do in the domain of intellect. The success of the Spanish arms in Italy reacted on Spanish literature, by bringing Spain more directly into contact with the new trend of human thought. The introduction of printing into Spain and the influence of the Renaissance are to the things of the mind events no less important than the discovery of the New World and the expulsion of the Moors. The contact with Italy was almost bound to affect the Spanish genius profoundly. And, as we shall see, it did.

Somewhere about the seed-time—the last decade or so of the fifteenth century (it is impossible to be more precise, in the absence of any exact record)—there was born at Barcelona a boy called Juan Boscá, Boscan in Spanish, who in the fullness of time was destined to become tutor to a lad famous—or, if it be preferred, infamous—in history as the great Duke of Alba. Boscan was not a genius, but he had a real taste for literature, a great intellectual curiosity, and the immitigable tenacity characteristic of the Catalans. Left to his own devices, he would probably have continued to write, as he did write, in the old accepted measures. Chance chose better for him by taking him to Granada in the summer of 1526; there he fell in with Andrea Navagero, the Venetian ambassador, and as to what passed between the two we have a first-hand account from Boscan himself who records it in an *Epístola a la Duquesa de Soma*, which is a prologue to the second and third books of his poems. In this letter, which is incidentally a literary manifesto, Boscan relates that Navagero pressed him to make the experiment of writing in the metres most in vogue in Italy. He goes on to say that to while away the dreary hours of his return journey, he tried his prentice hand at the new measures, found them amazingly difficult in their deliberate intricacy, and was so discouraged that he would have desisted had not Garci Lasso (as he says) 'animated me to persevere'— Garci Lasso whose 'sound judgement, not only in my opinion but in that of everybody, has been regarded as a leading principle of taste'. The combination of Boscan's tenacity and Garci Lasso's irresistible charm proved triumphant: between them the two men brought about a literary revolution, a revolution which caused no head to fall, though many heads were turned by it. Boscan lived longer than Garci Lasso de la Vega, was able to devote more time to literature, and left a greater body of verse: omitting his juvenile verses, written before his conversion by

Navagero, Boscan has left us over ninety sonnets, eleven *canciones*, and two epistles, not to speak of verbose paraphrases of Bernardo Tasso and Bembo. So far as natural endowment went, it is by no means clear that Boscan was superior to Francisco Imperial who first introduced Dante into Castilian. Boscan had not the poetic temperament in anything like the same degree as Santillana, who plumed himself on transplanting to Spanish soil the sonnet-form. Yes! he transplanted it, but was unable to acclimatize it there. Boscan had nothing approaching the intellectual and experimenting audacity of Juan de Mena; but though he made blunders of his own, he avoided the disaster which overwhelmed Mena. The fact remains that Boscan succeeded where more gifted predecessors had failed. How are we to explain his success which is all the more surprising inasmuch as Castilian was not his native tongue? I am not unaware that attempts are made to belittle this disadvantage. It may be argued that geographical proximity caused Cataluña to be more affected by Italian influence than any other part of the Peninsula. I am not unaware that Auzias March was an incorrigible Petrarchist. But, as regards Auzias March, whom Boscan translates in some of his poems, it must be remembered that he wrote in Catalan. The first allegation, that Italian influence was more deeply rooted in Boscan's native province than elsewhere, might go some way towards explaining Navagero's easy conversion of Boscan. It would not explain how he came to win so enduring a triumph in a language which was not his own. He did not make grammatical errors, but his ear was not of the finest, and he never contrived to dominate Castilian perfectly. That is what was meant by a younger contemporary, the altisonant Herrera, when, nearly half a century after the Catalan was in his grave, he reproached Boscan with 'remaining a foreigner in his language'. No: we must seek elsewhere for an explanation of Boscan's success.

There can be no reasonable doubt that this success was in great measure due to the conquering charm of his comrade, Garci Lasso de la Vega, whose poems were published posthumously in conjunction with his own, and continued to be so printed for many years. Thus in death Boscan received from Garci Lasso the same loyal support which had never failed him during life.

Nature had conspired with the blind power called chance to shower almost all the gifts on Garci Lasso. Between them, they could not give him happiness; but all else was added to him in abundance; illustrious descent, high position, imperial favour, incomparable charm, reckless valour, a superb presence, and, to crown all, a seductive genius. No name is more redolent of magic, more exquisitely appropriate to a delicate and glorious personality than the name of Garci Lasso de la Vega. Yet it is something of an accident that the poet was so called. His father had begun life as Garcia Suarez de Figueroa, and had afterwards assumed the surname of his maternal grandmother Elvira Lasso de la Vega. Surnames were only just coming into general use, and were employed rather capriciously. We see this exemplified in Garci Lasso's brothers. Garci Lasso's unabbreviated name was Garcia Lasso de la Vega y Guzman. One of his younger brothers was known as Gonzalo Ruiz de la Vega, another as Francisco de la Vega y Mendoza, a third as Fernando de Guzman. These are not negligible details; they not only illustrate the prevailing anarchy in these matters; a knowledge of them will facilitate the work of the investigator. He finds, for instance, that the verses to Urganda la Desconocida at the beginning of *Don Quixote* were adapted by Cervantes from a copy of caustic verses by a Dominican monk called Domingo de Guzman; it will interest him to know that this person was the third son of the poet with whom we are concerned.

Garci Lasso was born in 1503, lost his

father nine years later, was carefully educated, and at the age of seventeen was received into the household of Charles V (Charles I of Spain). It was probably in this way that he first became acquainted with Boscan, and with the future Duke of Alba. He attracted both of them as he attracted Charles V who appointed him *contino*—a post which appears to have corresponded to the position of personal aide-de-camp. He was soon to be tried severely. His elder brother, Pedro Lasso de la Vega, who is described by a hostile witness as a 'loyal knight, a lover of justice and the public good', sympathized with the popular movement which culminated in the rising of the *Comunidades*. Pedro appears to have exercised a restraining influence, but he failed to prevent an appeal to arms, and he felt bound to stand by those whom he had hitherto supported. Garci Lasso had to choose between his personal attachment to his brother, and his sense of public duty. He decided for the latter, served against the insurgents, and received at the battle of Olías a wound in the face which, however, did not mar his fine appearance personally. His heroic and unhesitating loyalty delighted Charles V, and henceforward his record is one of continuous and, on the whole, successful campaigns. He took part in the expedition to relieve Rhodes, fought in countless engagements against the French under Francis I, was made a Knight of the famous Order of Santiago in 1523, and received further promotion before being summoned to Flanders where he obtained still higher advancement. It was perhaps at Charles's instigation that in 1526 Garci Lasso married Elena Stúñiga, a lady-in-waiting to the Emperor's lovely consort, Isabel of Portugal. If so, the idea was not of the happiest. Garci Lasso's work is full of autobiographical touches, but it would require a microscopic eye to find in his bitter-sweet verses a single allusion to Elena Stúñiga. This cannot be explained away as a compliance with an artistic convention, for Garci Lasso's ally, Boscan, abounds with allusions to his domestic felicity. Garci Lasso was naturally much less reticent than Boscan, and his persistent mutism may be significant. What that significance amounts to it is not for me to determine.

Garci Lasso remained in Spain for some three years, and in 1529, after making his will (which was witnessed by Boscan), embarked at Barcelona for Italy to witness the formal coronation of Charles V at Bologna by the pontiff whose capital the imperial armies had recently sacked and pillaged. Garci Lasso was now in his real home, but he was not immediately free to dedicate himself to the cultivation of poetry, as he would have desired. He was sent to France on a special mission to Francis I, and, on his return to Italy some two years later, was dispatched to Germany and Austria with the Duke of Alba. An old indiscretion of his was now called up against him. Some time previously his nephew Garci Lasso (whose portrait has been accepted as that of his famous uncle) had been secretly married at Ávila to Isabel de la Cueva, niece of the Duke of Alburquerque, and lady-in-waiting to the Empress Isabel. The Empress and the Alburquerques were opposed to the match, and extorted from the Emperor a decree forbidding it. Garci Lasso stood by his nephew, was accused of hurrying on the marriage before the imperial decree could arrive, and was certainly a witness at the wedding. To cut a long story short, the Empress took deep offence at Garci Lasso's action, and though he escaped her resentment in Spain itself, he felt the weight of it in Germany. In company with Alba, he met the Emperor at Regensburg (Ratisbona), and was exiled to the Grosse-Schütt-Insel, a remote island in the Danube, mentioned in the poem beginning

Con un manso ruido
de agua corriente y clara
cerca el Danubio una isla, que pudiera

*ser lugar escogido
para que descansara
quien como yo estó agora no estuviera.*

In this unaccustomed and enforced tranquillity, Garci Lasso remained exiled (so it appears—he is not lavish of dates— a characteristic of other charming and poetical spirits) till the summer of 1532 when, no doubt through the influence of the Duke of Alba, he was released and sent to Naples, there to serve under the Viceroy, the Marqués de Villafranca, Alba's uncle. Naples we may henceforth regard as Garci Lasso's home, for though he was often called away from it—to Barcelona and perhaps to the Tunis campaign of 1535—his absences were relatively short, and he returned always with an infinite delight. We are well informed of Garci Lasso's stay in Naples, for it is the subject of an exhaustive and interesting monograph by Signor Croce who once concerned himself with Spanish literature before he succumbed to the fascination of philosophy. Among Garci

Lasso's Neapolitan friends he may well have counted the famous heterodox mystic, Juan Valdés, who had settled in the southern city some years before, away from the perilous attentions of the Spanish Inquisition; he probably knew such poets as Francesco Molza and Annibale Caro; and we know that he was on intimate terms with the poet Luigi Tansillo and with the scholarly Antonio Telesio, while he corresponded with Bembo who esteemed him as the greatest genius yet produced by Spain, one capable of surpassing all the other poets of Europe. 'Nothing that I have read in our time', says Bembo, 'has been characterized by greater elegance, simplicity and purity—and assuredly not by so much sublimity.' But he was not destined to remain lapped in this lettered ease, and enchanted calm. Charles V, irritated by the French forays and raids into Italian territories under his suzerainty, defied Francis I to single combat, and, when this challenge was not accepted, resolved on the invasion of

France. Garci Lasso formed part of the expedition. It was to be his last. All went well in this Provençal campaign of 1536 till the 13th of October when the Spanish forces found themselves 'held up' by a small body of marksmen in the fort of Muy, near Fréjus. This was not to be endured. The Spanish artillery was brought into action and speedily made a breach in the poor fortifications. There was some delay before the fort was stormed. Charles V lost patience, and expressed displeasure to those about him. Some report of the sovereign's dissatisfaction reached Garci Lasso, who was acting as *mestre del campo* (as who should say brigadier-general). Stung to the quick by the implied reproach, Garci Lasso resolved to lead the storming-party and, to be better seen by his men, he took off his helmet. To obtain more freedom of movement he likewise doffed his breastplate or cuirass. Racing along, he was among the first to reach the storming-ladders. But his temerity cost him dear.

The defenders rolled huge stones down on their assailants. Garci Lasso was mortally wounded, and fell back into the arms of two brother officers—one known to fame subsequently as the general of the Jesuits, St. Francis Borgia, the other perhaps being that mediocre versifier Jerónimo de Urrea--*buen caballero y mal poeta*—as Acuña afterwards called him. No doubt it is more pleasing to think of Urrea's devoted gallantry at Muy than of his detestable translation of the *Orlando furioso* which was too much for even Cervantes's illimitable indulgence.

Garci Lasso's life ended three weeks later. His work was done. That work was not voluminous in bulk. It consists of three eclogues, two elegies, five *canciones*, an epistle and some thirty-eight sonnets. This is not copious production, as production goes in Spain. But it is as much as we could expect from one who perished at the age of thirty-three and who could only snatch for composition such breathless intervals as occurred between two campaigns. As he himself says in his third eclogue, he wrote with the din of approaching battles in his ears, passing from sword to pen as he could:

Tomando ora la espada, ora la pluma.

Boscan had introduced the Italian *cancion, octavas rimas,* tercets and sonnets. He had also attempted blank verse; but his *versos sueltos* are frank failures. Góngora said with incisive exaggeration that he would as soon meet with a *buey suelto* as a *verso suelto* of Boscan's. It cannot be said that Garci Lasso's own blank verse is successful. It took a long while to master this recalcitrant measure, and on the whole it can scarcely be said to be congenial to the Spanish tongue. Garci Lasso has another failure to his account. In his second eclogue he introduces into his tercets some examples of the *rima percossa*—the rhyme in the middle of the hendecasyllabic—which he had borrowed from Sannazaro. The strain is too obvious and the attempt must be condemned. On the other hand, he outshines Boscan at every point in his *canciones* and in his sonnets. Some of these are among the most perfect yet written in Spanish. Take, for example, that which begins

O dulces prendas, por mi mal halladas,

an English version of which was published a hundred years ago by J. H. Wiffen (2), in the only English book, which, so far as I know, deals exclusively with Garci Lasso and his works.

Oh lovely gifts, by me too fatal found !
Lovely and dear indeed whilst Heaven was
    kind ;
In mine immortal memory ye are joined,
And sworn with her to give my dying
    wound ;
Who would have said, sweet seasons past,
    when crowned
With the ecstatic hope your emblems lent,
That one day you would have to represent
Despair so dark, affliction so profound?
Since in an hour ye made unpitying theft
Of those Elysian dreams, do not deny

To take as well the sorrows you have left;
Else, can I but suspect ye raised so high
My youthful joys, to wish that I should die
Midst mournful memories of the bliss
    bereft !

I am rather inclined to agree with Mr. Saintsbury that the hunting up of 'sources', the detection of possible plagiarisms may be overdone (perhaps he emphasizes a little too much, when he declares that such an occupation is about on the same level as cat-hunting). Garci Lasso has, like Tennyson, suffered a good deal at the hands of these zealots from the time of Sanchez onwards. Still, there can be no great harm in pointing out that the opening of this sonnet (which bears the number ten in most recent editions of Garci Lasso) is manifestly suggested by a passage in the *Aeneid*, book 4 :

Dulces exuviae, dum fata deusque sinebant.

This is not noted in the latest annotated edition of Garci Lasso which I have seen : that edited by Tomás Navarro Tomás. I hope that I shall not incur the censure of my friend Mr. Saintsbury, if I attempt to remedy the omission.

This leads us to two general questions: that of Garci Lasso's originality and that of the value of the changes for which, even more than Boscan, I think he shares the responsibility. It is perfectly true that Garci Lasso is extremely derivative. His debts to Sannazaro are unconcealed and palpable: the whole idea of his eclogues is taken from the *Arcadia*, and in some few cases the paraphrase of Sannazaro's expression is startlingly close. In his sonnets he draws largely on Petrarch, the inevitable model of all ambitious sonneteers. He embodies thoughts austere from Dante, and in a lighter mood he borrows material from his friend Tansillo. Bembo is not too precious for him, Virgil is not too stately, Horace is not too gaily wise, and Martial is not too laconic and incisive. Garci Lasso takes freely with both hands, what he contributes is his own rare temperament, his melancholy vision of beauty, his morbid susceptibility, his subjective transcription of an ineffable dream. To him his dreams were real, and he is content to transmit his illusions to the reader who falls within the circle ruled by the enchanter's wand. We obey because we must: even as Caliban obeyed Prospero. It is difficult to see how Garci Lasso could have acted otherwise than he did. He had to introduce new metres, no doubt. But that was only a small part of his self-assigned task. He had at the same time to create an entire *corpus* of poetry which should correspond in substance to the new vehicle of expression. His metrical dexterity is astounding. Take, for instance, the famous *Cancion a la flor de Gnido* in which the rhymes follow in this sequence: *a b a b b*. The measure is taken from Bernardo Tasso, but it is conveyed with such adroitness that the elder Tasso's claim to priority has been forgotten for nearly three centuries, and the importation—called a *lira* from the only noun in the first line—has been universally recognized, even in Italy itself, as an authentic Spanish product. So much so, that it has taken permanent root in Spain, and has been reproduced, without any change, however trivial, by so consummate an artist as Luis de Leon and by so inspired a singer as St. John of the Cross. To have imposed a mode of versification on two minds so aloof from mundane influences, so independent in essence, so appreciative of celestial melody, is indeed a remarkable achievement which vindicates Garci Lasso's procedure. He had clearly established a new standard of beauty.

This leads us to the second of our questions. Striking a rough balance of profit and loss, were the changes introduced by Boscan and Garci Lasso advisable or not? The question is what is called academic (by which I do not mean —what is so often meant—imbecile): it has no practical bearing, for the decision has been definitely taken and there is no going back on it, but it has a speculative interest. No change in human affairs does half as much good as its partisans hope or its opponents fear. Scarcely any change but results in some loss: how was it with the adoption in Spain of the Italian metrical system? The old moulds of literature were outworn, and needed renovation: even Castillejo, the soul and brain of the opposition to Boscan, admitted that. By acquaintance with new models, the younger school of Spanish poets acquired the classic qualities of serenity and dignity. It is far from clear that they, or the generation which came after them, did not lose something of their native originality, their keen sincerity. Henceforward there is for some time an appreciable separation between lyric poetry and the facts of life. Lyrical poetry was more concerned with the artificialities of the pastoral convention than with the realities which shook the world to its foundations. The personal hatreds which inspired often the verses of Santillana were banished, and that was no doubt a gain. But other things were likewise under a ban: the deepest problems over which men contended in pamphlets or in pulpits, or for which they died on the field of battle. Lyrical poetry took no note of the events which changed the face of the world, and spent itself on the adaptation of mythological stories, on the presentation of dignified shepherds and lovely shepherdesses, in the construction of pictures wherein, as Núñez de Arce, himself an accomplished poet of our time, said, 'everything is falsified, heaven and earth, men and nature alike'.

There is much more than a grain of truth in these bitter reproaches of Núñez de Arce's. But they touch Garci Lasso's imitators most closely: they do not apply to Garci Lasso himself. He is still the 'Prince of Poets' as was his contemporary Ronsard in France. And his reputation has never undergone such ups and downs as Ronsard's. I happen to know from Núñez de Arce that he always considered

Garci Lasso as a great spirit and wonderful artificer in words. Perhaps that would not be said of Ronsard by any competent French critic who had outgrown the influence of the generation of 1830. Possibly there are points of resemblance between some of Ronsard's compositions and some of Garci Lasso's : compare, for instance, the admirable sonnet : *Quand vous serez bien vieille,* or the no less famous ode : *Mignonne, allons voir si la rose,* with the poem beginning *En tanto que de rosa y azucena.* Such general semblances, purely accidental, no doubt, are not, I think, wholly obscured in the following version (3) :

As, love, the lily and purpureal rose
Show their sweet colours on thy chaste
    warm cheek,
Thy radiant looks, angelically meek,
Serene the tempest to divine repose,
And as thy hair, which for its birthright chose
The opal's dye, upon the whitest neck
Waved by the winds of heaven without
    a check,
In exquisite disorder falls and flows ;

Gather the rich fruit of thy mirthful spring,
Ere angry Time around thy temples shed
The snows of hasting age, his icy wing
Will wither the fresh rose, however red;
And changing not his custom, quickly change
The glory of all objects in his range.

If the resemblance exist, and is not accidental, the copyist is not Garci Lasso who died when Ronsard was twelve. Now Garci Lasso is often reproached with little Italian exoticisms, amounting to incorrections, and the same charge, perhaps with more justice, has been levelled against Cervantes. It may very well be that during their residence in Naples Garci Lasso, and Cervantes after him, picked up a few Italian idioms which clung to them like burrs. It may be that Garci Lasso, knowing his compositions would be read first of all by Italians— poets, cardinals, knights, and great ladies —was not as scrupulous in revision as he would otherwise have been. We cannot feel sure that Garci Lasso did not take a half-perverse, half-coquettish pleasure in introducing Italianisms as he would, at need, insert at the end of a Spanish poem a line entire from one of Petrarch's *canzoni*, for the sake of achieving a difficult rhyme, as, for instance, in the alembicated sonnet beginning *Con ansia extrema de mirar que tiene.*

So far as vocabulary goes, Garci Lasso strikes us by his unaffected speech and genuine modernity. His disadvantages are of another order. We cannot catch his multiple allusions, the point of which was plain to most educated contemporaries: these now need explanation in an elaborate commentary which few could write and fewer still are tempted to undertake as they believe the public to be too indolent, or at least too incurious, to read it. Garci Lasso suffers most from the disrepute into which the pastoral *genre* has fallen: but his undoubted greatness is plain to all who have an inkling of the principles of historical criticism. To estimate what he did for Spanish poetry we must compare the work of his predecessors at their best with that of his successors at their best. He asks a little too much of his readers, he expects everybody to know the name of Phaeton's sister and the name of the river by which she sat down and wept; he takes it for granted that everybody knows that Calisto is another name for the Great Bear. These are not pedantic affectations. He lived so much in an artificial world that it became to him a reality while the concrete world about him was a repugnant nightmare. In that ideal world he breathes, moves, and has his being. But perhaps his greatest charm is his gift of dulcet melody. To this, naturally, only Spaniards or those with a considerable knowledge of Spanish are susceptible. And perhaps this accounts for the relative neglect of him outside Spain. It is true that he is mentioned (with Boscan) by Du Bartas, and Abraham Fraunce has a perfunctory allusion to him (and to Boscan) in *The Arcadian Rhetorike*; he was translated in a futile and fragmentary way by François de Belleforest in the *Pastorale amoureuse*, and in a still more unsatisfactory fashion by Drummond of Hawthornden who apparently ranked Garci Lasso and Boscan on the same level. The Spaniards made no such mistake. Garci Lasso's poems had been issued originally with those of Boscan, whose widow was zealous for the reputation of her late husband and his friend. That friend's fame grew apace and a separate edition of Garci Lasso's poems appeared in 1570 while another was published by Sanchez, *el Brocense*, in 1577. Since then his superiority has been universally recognized: Garci Lasso is in Spanish poetry what he was in real life: a matchless and starry paladin. Spain still abides by his methods and still cherishes the memory of the elfin notes of his inspired music. When we survey the interminable battalions of his followers, we cannot think of him as of

> a dreamer that slumbers
> And a singer that sings no more.

TWO MYSTIC POETS

It may seem a violent transition to pass from Garci Lasso's light and deliberate paganism to the intense and glowing ardour of such enraptured spirits as Santa Teresa and St. John of the Cross. If there is a contrast between the elegant paladin and the two saints, chronology must take the blame for it. But it is possible that the contrast is not so marked as appears at first sight. In the intervals of innumerable campaigns, Garci Lasso built for himself an ideal world, and dwelt in a land of pastoral visions, lulled by echoes of Virgilian music which came to him muffled through sylvan glades of his own imagining. The two saints lived even more remote from the material world which encompassed them; raised far above all mundane passions, and all earthly aims, they constantly beheld through the transparent curtain of their vehement dreams the celestial choirs and the asphodels of paradise. There are points of contact between the studious art of Garci Lasso de la Vega and the ineffable music of St. John of the Cross. But we need not anticipate the order of events. Santa Teresa comes first in point of time, and to her our first remarks must be devoted.

The general outline of her history is familiar to most, and need not be traced minutely. Her name in the world was Teresa de Cepeda y Ahumada. She was born at Ávila on March 28, 1515. She was not cast into an atmosphere of morbid pietism. Her ancestors were mostly fighting men: of her seven brothers, six were soldiers who made a name for themselves in the New World. 'My father', says the saint, 'was very much given to the reading of good books'; her mother, she says in another passage, was much addicted to reading books of chivalry.

Brought up in this atmosphere, it is not surprising that in collaboration with her brother Rodrigo, she should have written a chivalresque romance in her childhood. It would have been interesting to know how the saint, in this crude juvenile effort, disposed of her invincible knights and charming ladies, her colossal giants and astute dwarfs. But the childish effort has not survived, though we are informed that those who read it thought it extremely ingenious. This is not very credible, for it is precisely the ingenious note which is lacking in Santa Teresa's maturer work. She was soon called away from these early excursions into literature. Good man as he was, her father had no notion of playing the part of Jephthah the Gileadite in however modified a form, and when Teresa wished to enter the Carmelite Convent of the Incarnation at Ávila, he strenuously opposed the project. He resigned himself to the inevitable when the girl, though only sixteen, ran away from home in 1531.

The rest of her life may be followed in a score of books in which her practical sense, her adroit diplomacy, her organizing faculties are duly celebrated. For those more interested in her solitary and enthusiastic youth, with its alternations of dejection and buoyancy of spirit, the drama of her checks, victories and indomitable struggles-- these may be best read in that fascinating autobiography which was never intended for the public eye. In the *Libro de su vida*, in the *Libro de las Fundaciones*, and in her copious correspondence we see the 'wonderful woman' in every aspect of her multiform character: confidential in the *Libro de su vida*; intellectual and aloof in the *Libro de las Fundaciones*; personal, reproving, encouraging, cajoling, maternal—perhaps even a little fussy —in her innumerable letters. One derives from these three sources the impression that she combines in an extraordinary degree a practical faculty and positive sense with a power of subjective

TWO MYSTIC POETS

vision and poetic imagination. This singular combination of gifts, apparently incompatible, constitutes the rare originality of her genius and has for us a more permanent interest than her practical talent. Others might have reformed a religious order, others might have founded seventeen convents and fifteen monasteries. No one but Santa Teresa could have written the *Camino de perfeccion*, the *Conceptos del amor de Dios*, and, above all, the *Moradas* or *Castillo interior*. Here she deserves the epithet, so often applied to her, of 'our seraphic mother', here she recounts the amazing spiritual adventures of her lofty and romantic spirit, here she condenses all her unparalleled experiences of the inner life, leading her readers onwards step by step through the seven vestibules of her mystic castle till she conducts them at last to the ultimate annihilation of self and absorption in the Divine Essence.

Luckily for the world, her manuscripts came into the hands of Luis de Leon, himself a great writer, who instantly recognized a spirit akin to his own. He treated them with the most profound respect, always reading them, as he tells us, with increased admiration, never modifying a word, collating all copies with their originals, esteeming that in many passages he perceived a superhuman talent. In these mystic masterpieces, the saint reveals herself as a poet. She is never so much a poet as when she writes in prose. Her style is the expression of her unique personality. She turns away from art, she eschews rhetoric. Her vocabulary, varied, supple, and archaic (even at the time when she used it) is a model of the speech of the best society in Old Castile. You may find writers more correct, more elegant, more skilful in marshalling battalions of insubordinate words: you will only find in Spanish literature one writer who equals her in graphic force and in convincing simplicity. And it is that common trait—the trait of exquisite naturalness—which has led

TWO MYSTIC POETS

Froude to place Santa Teresa on the same level as Cervantes. Like Cervantes, Santa Teresa was a poet: but a poet only in prose. Both were poets who lacked the accomplishment of verse. She implicitly rejects the title of a poet in her *Vida* where, referring obviously to herself, she says: 'I know one who, though not a poet, improvized certain stanzas, heartfelt and expressive of her pain. They were not the product of her own understanding; but to enjoy more keenly that bliss which so sweet a pain caused her, she complained of it in that way to God'. The saint wrote verses very sparingly, not more than fourteen or fifteen poems have survived, perhaps not as many as a dozen, if we choose to be exacting as to evidence for authenticity. She burst into song on rare occasions, spontaneously, much as a blithe child will sing a simple song in sheer light-heartedness. It is as though 'the morning stars sang together', as though we had fragments of the mysterious song in the Book of the

Revelation (xiv. 3) that none could learn ' but the hundred and forty and four thousand, which were redeemed from the earth'. The saint never enters upon the province of conscious art; she had a horror of rhetoric which would have commended her to Verlaine; her natural taste was for the simpler popular forms as in the Shepherd's Carol: *Hoy nos viene a redimir*, well Englished by Mr. Arthur Symons: (4)

> To-day, a shepherd and our kin,
> O Gil, to ransom us is sent,
> And he is God Omnipotent.
>
> For us hath He cast down the pride
> And prison wall of Satanas;
> But He is of the kin of Bras,
> Of Menga, also of Llorent.
> O is not God Omnipotent?
>
> If He is God, how then is He
> Come hither and here crucified?
> —With His dying sin also died,
> Enduring death the innocent,
> Gil, how is God Omnipotent!

TWO MYSTIC POETS

Why, I have seen Him born, pardie,
And of a most sweet shepherdess.
—If He is God, how can He be
With such poor folk as these content?
—Seest not He is Omnipotent?

Give over idle parleyings,
And let us serve Him, you and I,
And since He came on earth to die,
Let us die with Him too, Llorent,
For He is God Omnipotent.

This little carol in dialogue exhibits Santa Teresa in a most characteristic mood. I am not unaware that the authenticity of this poem has been questioned. But I think I can reassure you on that head, for an autograph copy of the first three stanzas in the saint's handwriting has recently been discovered in Florence. The absence of the fourth stanza need not perplex us, nor exclude the simple little poem from the canon. For the saint never troubled to collect her verses, and was not always able to remember them. For instance, in writing to her brother, Lorenzo de Cepeda (January 2, 1577), she mentions a poem of hers '*O hermosura que excedéis*', quotes three stanzas and then breaks off with the remark: 'I do not remember any more.'

Her personal taste was all for the popular forms of verse; but she was the child of her own time, and, being born at the beginning of the sixteenth century, just as she had a liking for *Amadis de Gaula*, she had a weakness for the alembicated songs of the *Cancioneros*. Doubtless, like her disciple Catalina de Jesús, she delighted in the celebrated lines of Escrivá—*Ven muerte tan escondida*—admired by Cervantes and by Calderon. Some echo of them and perhaps of some verses by Francisco Lopez de Villalobos may be caught in Santa Teresa's poem beginning:

Vivo sin vivir en mi,
y tan alta vida espero,
que muero porque no muero.

I do not say that these lines are the most

typical of the saint's usual manner; they are more subtle than she is apt to be in verse, and are an interesting anticipation of the *conceptismo* represented by Quevedo and Gracian in the following century. At any rate, this composition, written at Salamanca in 1571, as we know from the saint's colleague Sor Isabel de Jesús, is the most famous of all Santa Teresa's verses; much of it is known by heart throughout the peninsula, and its wide popularity is such that its inclusion imposes itself on the most autocratic anthologist. It is generally known as Santa Teresa's 'Gloss'; and, as far as I know, there does not exist any adequate rendering of the poem in English.

Santa Teresa died on October 4, 1582 at the age of 67, having been professed for nearly 46 years, the first twenty-six of which she spent as a nun in the convent of the Incarnation at Ávila and the remaining twenty as foundress of the Discalced Carmelites, an occupation which took her over a great part of Spain. We know from the Book of *Proverbs* (xiii. 15) that 'good understanding giveth favour, but the way of transgressors is hard'. The way of reformers is not always precisely smooth, as Santa Teresa was to learn by experience. She had—need it be said?—to face the opposition of clerics, banded together by bishops and headed by a timid booby who held the position of Papal Nuncio. She had to contend with the caprices of great ladies who seemed at times to confuse levity with devotion.

She was regarded with suspicion by the straiter sects of Pharisees who made the most of her little humorous sallies, as when she rebuked a young nun who showed a tendency to indulge in excessive austerities. The saint's reproof 'Obedience, my daughter—and a rasher of bacon' is a phrase which has passed into something like a proverb. Moreover, at almost every stage, her proceedings were viewed with jealous eyes by the Inquisition. On the other hand, she was not without friends in high places. She was most fortunate in making the acquaintance of a Carmelite monk, whose name was Juan de Yepes, but who was known in his order, and is now famous the whole world overlong, as San Juan de la Cruz. She formed a redoubtable alliance with San Juan de la Cruz, a man of resplendent gifts, twenty-seven years younger than herself, consumed by the same reforming passion and endowed with a mystic fervour no less zealous and concentrated. It may be that St. John of the Cross had less diplomatic tact than Santa Teresa; it may be that harsher measures were deliberately adopted against him. Be that as it may, he suffered bitter persecution, and died in most distressing circumstances before he was fifty years of age. Santa Teresa's regard for St. John of the Cross, apart from her esteem for his eminent sanctity, was, as Churton observes, like that of an experienced mother for a son of the most splendid promise. That describes the position accurately. As she was the Mother, so is he in a sense the Father, of the great Carmelite reform; or, to word it differently, what she did for the Carmelite nuns, he did for the friars of the order.

Perhaps inferior to Santa Teresa in mundane experience, scarcely equal to her, it may be, in practical organizing talent, St. John of the Cross was much more copiously endowed with respect to absolute literary gifts. Santa Teresa would no doubt have felt flattered could she have known that in the 1912 edition of the *Llama de amor viva* the last five stanzas of her *letrilla* are described as an original poem by St. John of the Cross. This ascription cannot, however, be accepted. As it happens, and as might be expected, St. John of the Cross frequently refers to works of Santa Teresa's long before such works were printed: it could hardly be otherwise, if he referred to them at all, for only one composition of Santa Teresa's was published before her death, which occurred nine years before his. But there is another consideration which, I think you will admit, is decisive: it is, I submit, fatal to the theory that even any part of the *letrilla* which bears Santa Teresa's name can really have been the work of St. John of the Cross. Apart from the fact that the *letrilla* is curiously unlike the authentic poems of St. John of the Cross, we are informed by that unimpeachable witness, Sor Isabel de Jesús, that the *letrilla* was written by Santa Teresa in 1571. Now, by a lucky chance, the holograph copy of the *Llama de amor viva* is still in existence, and it proves to be dated 1584—that is to say, two years after Santa Teresa's death. This circumstance must be taken in conjunction with the testimony of Sor Isabel de Jesús, with the explicit statement of the Teresian biographer Yepes, and with the implicit evidence of the *Vida*, of the *Castillo interior*, and of the *Conceptos del amor de Dios*. It might be possible to contend that no single one of these considerations, taken above, is conclusive. That may, or may not, be so. But these considerations do not stand alone. They are, each and all, corroborative and supplementary, and nobody who has any idea of what evidence is can deny that their cumulative force is almost irresistible. It may be as well to emphasize this point, as there are some curious notions afloat as to what evidence is, and is not, in such matters. I do not think that I am putting the matter too high if I say that the combination of circumstances which I have laid before you is significant enough to render all further discussion absolutely futile. It is conceivable, no doubt, that St. John of the Cross might possibly have written the *letrilla* which bears Santa Teresa's name. But that is not the point. What we are discussing is whether he wrote it or not, whether there is any solid ground for rejecting a traditional ascription which is supported by irrefragable contemporary evidence, or not. It would add little to the glory of St. John of the Cross if he were shown to have written the *letrilla*— except indeed that it would prove him to be a trifle more versatile than had hitherto been suspected. It would also prove him to have departed farther than we have any reason to suppose from the literary standards to which he seems steadfastly to have adhered. He may have done these things. If so, we ask for evidence that he did. It is not forthcoming.

St. John of the Cross was not learned, if judged by any very high standard of learning. But he was more versed in mundane literature than Santa Teresa, and the very form of his poems betrays the influence of Garci Lasso de la Vega. It is one of art's little ironies that the form of the *lira*, first used by Garci Lasso for the very human purpose of softening an Italian beauty's heart, should have recommended itself above all others to St. John of the Cross, as the most appropriate form of expression for his ecstatic exaltations. There is an excellent version of his *Llama de amor viva* by Mr. Arthur Symons,(5) which suggests a parallel between the amorous pleading of Garci Lasso and what has been daringly called the 'celestial eroticism' of St. John of the Cross :

O Flame of living love,
That dost eternally
Pierce through my soul with so consuming heat,
Since there's no help above,
Make thou an end of me,
And break the bond of this encounter sweet.

O burn that burns to heal!
O more than pleasant wound!
And O soft hand, O touch most delicate,
That dost new life reveal,
That dost in grace abound,
And, slaying, dost from death to life translate!

O lamps of fire that shined
With so intense a light
That those deep caverns where the senses live,
Which were obscure and blind,
Now with strange glories bright,
Both heat and light to His belovèd give!

TWO MYSTIC POETS

With how benign intent
Rememberest thou my breast,
Where thou alone abidest secretly;
And in thy sweet ascent,
With glory and good possessed,
How delicately thou teachest love to me!

St. John of the Cross accompanies his poems by an elaborate and voluminous commentary in prose. This commentary —now scholastically ingenious in the manner of the mediaeval schoolmen and now exuberantly oriental owing to its wealth of Biblical reminiscence—is intended (we are told) as a guide to highly trained confessors, expert casuists, deeply versed in the baffling arcana of moral theology. It is a relief to know this. The prose commentary of St. John of the Cross is incomprehensible to at least one layman whom I, for obvious personal reasons, would wish to regard as a person of average intelligence. And he is not alone. The prose of St. John of the Cross is of extreme obscurity to the profane. Quevedo and Estébanez Calderon pass as being two of the most difficult authors in Spanish literature; the difficulty of both the seventeenth- and the nineteenth-century authors is very real, but both are simpler than is St. John of the Cross in his prose commentary on himself. In the cases of Quevedo and Estébanez Calderon, the difficulties concerned with grammar and vocabulary, can, with application, be surmounted. St. John of the Cross moves on a lofty, inaccessible plane, breathing an atmosphere too rarefied for the ordinary mortal. In verse, unobscured by his too subtle commentary, he is infinitely more comprehensible than in his prose. It is customary to say that he sings with the voice of an angel. That may be. For me it is enough to describe his achievement in terms of literature. His poems are of irreproachable technique; they abound in daring oriental images; they stir you with their enchanting music, they are irresistible in the force of their emotional appeal. St. John of the Cross has not the romantic personality of Santa

Teresa; he has not her caressing beauty of phrase in prose. But he is a far greater poet and, in his own special sphere, he has no equal in Spanish literature.

LOPE DE VEGA

THE average non-expert reader quite rightly brackets the names of Cervantes and Lope de Vega together. But, whereas he has a fairly accurate idea of Cervantes's life and achievements, he has but the mistiest impression of Lope de Vega whom he knows solely by report as the author of nearly two thousand plays. It is true that Lope de Vega is most famous as a marvellously prolific dramatist; but he was much more than that. He left no department of literature unattempted, and for a long while he was convinced that his fame would rest upon his poems: not upon the plays which he dashed off in such breathless haste and left unrevised. He was mistaken, as we know. But his mistake was not unnatural: he esteemed most what cost him most effort and, while he improvised (so to say) his plays, he spent endless labour on filing and re-polishing improvised poems which are now read by few but experts. Lope de Vega has not Cervantes's universal appeal; but on that account he is more characteristically Spanish. And his personality, though less epical than Cervantes's in many respects, is not less romantic. For a long while—for over two hundred years after Lope de Vega's death—we were in the dark about his history, dependent for our knowledge on the record of his favourite Perez de Montalban, Quevedo's *bête noire*. The researches of the last half-century or so, especially of the last thirty years, have brought to light much new material. This new material compels us to conclude that Perez de Montalban deliberately misrepresented many facts and suppressed others, to such an extent that it has become necessary to rewrite the biography of Lope anew. This must be my excuse for briefly reviewing the established facts, so far as we know them, up to the present.

Born at Madrid on November 25, 1562, Lope de Vega was a man of the people. In after-years he took to signing himself Lope Felix de Vega Carpio, and Carpio was undoubtedly one of the names of his father Felix de Vega Carpio. Carpio is a name illustrious in Spanish mythology, and, to judge by the gorgeous escutcheon which Lope reproduces in some of his works, he was not unwilling to have it believed that he was, in some roundabout way, connected with that fabulous hero Bernardo del Carpio. Still, he did not try to conceal the fact that the Carpios had come down in the world by his father's time. His father is variously described as a lace-weaver or a basket-maker. The family came from Asturias, and (especially in the sixteenth century) an Asturian was presumptively noble. Lope was educated at the Theatine school and was there soon recognized to be a marvellous little boy. We need not believe all the stories told about him: that before he could write he composed verses which elder boys took down at his dictation, receiving part of his breakfast in payment of their help. Another story of his youth is that, at about the age of ten or so, he determined to see the world, cajoled a school-fellow into running away with him, and got as far as Segovia before he was arrested by the police who ignominiously bundled the runaways home again. There is nothing incredible in this tale: other lads, before and after Lope, have made away from school and it is not to be gainsaid that the marvellous boy is likely to have been a bit of a scapegrace. It is rarer for a boy not yet in his teens to translate a Latin poet into good vernacular verse. We still have Lope's poetical rendering of Claudian's *De raptu Proserpinae*, and if the date attached to it (1572) is authentic, the performance is remarkable for a boy of ten. Lope himself tells us that he began to write plays at the age of twelve, and his first piece, *El verdadero amante*, afterwards represented with success, still survives. It is not one of

Lope's best productions: but it is not his worst, and we can see in it an adumbration of his extraordinary gifts.

After leaving school, Lope was admitted, as page, to the household of the Bishop of Ávila. The Bishop took a liking to the wonderful youth, determined to give him a chance in the world, and sent him to the University of Alcalá. Lope would not seem to have been a very distinguished undergraduate, for his name is not to be found in any of the University registers. Always erratic and undisciplined, he enlisted in 1581-2, fought at the Azores, and on his return obtained a post as secretary to a noble. This brings us down to 1583. Lope was well enough thought of to be complimented by Cervantes in the *Galatea*. What he was best known for, at this time, was a series of *romances* in which he celebrates the charms of a certain Filis. This 'Filis' was known in real life as Elena Osorio, the daughter of a theatrical manager called Jerónimo Velazquez. But the course of this love-affair did not run smoothly. Elena Osorio preferred somebody else. Lope de Vega resented being jilted, and penned a series of disagreeable epigrams on the inconstant fair and her father. These amounted to what the law calls criminal libel; Lope was duly brought to trial, and condemned to be exiled from Madrid for eight years and from Castile for two years. If he disregarded the order of the Court by returning to Madrid before the eight years were out he was to go to the galleys; if he entered Castile within two years, he was to be put to death.

Lope feigned compliance and went for a short while to Valencia. The story runs that he returned thence to Madrid and straightway risked his head by eloping with Isabel de Urbina, daughter of a well-known King-at-arms. Such insolent defiance took the police by surprise, but they were soon on the traces of the fugitives. Lope married the lady by proxy on May 10, 1588—three months after his conviction—and embarked at Lisbon on the *San Juan*, a vessel which formed part of the Invincible Armada. He fought his way up the Channel and had his brother killed beside him. He used, so he tells us, the paper on which his love-verses to 'Filis' were written, as gun-wads. But he had not abandoned literature. When not actually sleeping or fighting, he was in his bunk at work on *La Hermosura de Angélica*, an epic of 11,000 lines which he published some fourteen years afterwards. On his return to Spain, he was employed as secretary to the fifth Duke of Alba, and subsequently to other great nobles, among them the Marqués de Sarriá, famous by his later title of the 'Conde de Lemos', as the patron of Cervantes.

All this while, Lope was writing for the stage, and getting no good by it. He anticipated Byron's view (a view which they both abandoned later) that no gentleman would, or could, accept payment for writing. Hence Lope's purse remained

LOPE DE VEGA

empty. After the death of his wife in 1595, his escapades were so numerous and flagrant that they got him into trouble with the law. The least culpable of these entanglements was one with the celebrated actress Micaela de Lujan, the Camila Lucinda of many of Lope's sonnets, and the mother of two very gifted children, Marcela, afterwards a nun, and Lope Felix del Carpio y Lujan. Both of these inherited much of their father's marvellous faculty.

The year 1598 saw Lope launched on a formal literary career (he did not regard plays as literature!) as the author of an epic poem, *La Dragontea*, and of a pastoral novel, *Arcadia*. In *La Dragontea* Lope takes the patriotic Spanish view of the exploits of *el Draque*—Drake—the dragon of the *Dragontea*. Now I may be wrong, but to me the best thing in the *Dragontea* is its intensely national point of view. Considering that Lope had been chased up the Channel by Drake, and considering that Drake had been a thorn in the side of Spain for about thirty years, it would have been amazing had Lope treated him tenderly. As a matter of fact, he pillories Drake, but it is difficult to resent these political prejudices of three centuries ago. The *Dragontea* does not fail to interest because of its political bias, but because the allegorical passages are wearisome, and because there is no light and shade in the presentation. The monotony of the diatribe becomes a bore, and few there are in Spain who have read the *Dragontea*. Even a sense of duty is not sufficient incentive. Still the *Dragontea* had some success at the time, and it went into several editions for the second of which Cervantes, then on good terms with the author, wrote a eulogistic sonnet. Cervantes is often praised as having English sympathies. Perhaps. But, evidently, he drew the line at Sir Francis Drake.

In the *Arcadia* as in most other pastoral novels, real personages are represented under feigned names. This no doubt gave to the book a special interest for contemporary readers, but that interest has long since died away. We know that Anfriso is the fifth Duke of Alba, and that Lope himself is Belardo. But these are about the only names that mean anything to us nowadays, and if there existed an annotated edition of the *Arcadia*, with plausible identifications of the other characters in the novel, I doubt if even experts would be enraptured at having the unmanageable key thrust into their hands. Another event important for Lope belongs to the year 1598. On May 3, he married again. His second wife was Juana de Guardo, daughter of a wealthy pork-packer. This exposed Lope to the taunt of having married for money, and some biting verses—one copy is by Góngora—formulate the charge not obscurely. There seems to be no foundation for it. If Lope calculated on profiting financially by his marriage, he was greatly mistaken, for his father-in-law was a notorious miser, as Lope must have known by common repute. Not a farthing did Lope receive. His second marriage was apparently one of affection, and the influence of Juana de Guardo on her husband was wholly for good. His industry at this period was prodigious. In 1599 he issued his *Isidro*, a poem in *quintillas*, in honour of St. Isidore—not the great St. Isidore of Seville, but the humbler saint of Madrid. Lope, as may be recalled, had landed from the Armada expedition with the MS. of *La Hermosura de Angélica*. He expected great things from this, continued polishing it for fourteen years and brought it out in 1602, bound up with two hundred sonnets as a complementary postscript. These sonnets contain some of Lope's best and most sincere work. The *Isidro* had displayed his liking for the native popular *quintillas*; he now proved his versatility by appearing as an *italianizante* in *La Hermosura de Angélica*, where he is bold enough to compete with Ariosto's *Orlando furioso*. The *Orlando* remains: the *Hermosura de Angélica* looks rather wan beside it, but there are fine passages, unfortunately overlaid by innumerable digressions which were always Lope's snare.

His diligence was unflagging. Undiscouraged by the fact that he had not eclipsed Ariosto, he published in 1604 a miscellaneous volume entitled *El Peregrino en su patria.* So far as I know, this was the only work of Lope's done into English in his life-time, but the book is valued by bibliographers of the stage, for it contains a list of all the plays written by Lope up to 1603. The list gives the titles of 220 plays, but perhaps we ought not to put our trust in it too blindly, for Lope omits some plays, duplicates others, and altogether proves himself an indifferent arithmetician. *El Peregrino en su patria* has brought on me some unnecessary correspondence which I somewhat regret. You will remember that in *Wild Wales* George Borrow talks of Lope rather at random as the author of the 'best ghost-story in the world', and though I am not Borrow's executor—I never saw him in my life—some few dozen people write to me annually to know where the story occurs. To look for a specific passage in Lope is rather like hunting for a needle in a bundle of hay. However, in case any of you are ever asked for the reference, you may be glad to have it now. The story occurs in *El Peregrino en su patria*: it is, as the Spaniards would say, *espeluznante* (hair-raising in its accumulated horrors), but it is very far from deserving Borrow's praise. Not that Borrow was insincere: he took the trouble to translate the story into English, and his version is duly printed in the second volume of Knapp's *Life of Borrow*.

But prose could not win Lope de Vega away from the attractions of verse. Writing the same year, he published under the title of *Rimas* (1604) a re-impression of his sonnets as well as some minor compositions, unequal indeed, but at their best distinguished for their grace and natural beauty. In *La Hermosura de Angélica* Lope had been bold enough to measure himself against Ariosto. The *italianizante* in him was irrepressible. His ambition was not satisfied. It remained for him to outshine Tasso, and this he attempted in the *Jerusalen conquistada* which he styled a tragic epic. The epical spirit flickers rather feebly in the *Jerusalen*, and Tasso withstands the onset. What Lope has written is a rhymed historical narrative, facile, fluent, lavish in rather gaudy embellishments. Perhaps the most interesting thing in the *Jerusalen conquistada* is the announcement on the title-page that Lope was in 1609 a Familiar of the Inquisition. Apparently he was passing through a pietistic phase at this time, for between 1609 and 1611 he enrolled himself in three religious confraternities. In 1611 an attempt was made on Lope's life: so, at least, he avows and I see no reason to doubt him, for he had made a large number of enemies, either by his triumphs on the stage or by the excesses of his conduct. In 1612 he produced that wondrous masterpiece, partly in prose and partly in verse, *Los Pastores de Belen*, an absolute marvel of beauty and devotion: the only defect of which is that it is far too long. If it were less diffuse, however, it would not be so typically Spanish as it is.

This year of 1612 Lope suffered a heavy blow by the death of his son Carlos Felix to whom he was profoundly attached; next year (August 13, 1613) the boy's mother followed him. Lope was a second time a widower. His pietistic tendencies deepened, and early in 1614 he was ordained priest. By taking orders he committed an irreparable mistake. Orthodox enough in all essentials, he had sunk into a series of scandalous intrigues which were the talk of the town. Unluckily for him his private correspondence at this period has been preserved, and this presents Lope in a most unfavourable light: we see him talking loosely, writing loosely, thinking loosely, acting loosely, with no sort of recognition of the gravity of the irrevocable step which he was taking. Even before he was ordained, he should have realized that he was blundering in the dark. His intentions may have been the best in the world.

But habit was too strong for him. He could not reform radically in twenty-four hours. There is a disagreeable allusion to him in the preface to the Second Part of *Don Quixote*: Cervantes, with whom he had quarrelled, refers to him ironically as a Familiar of the Inquisition, notorious for his 'virtuous occupation.' His repute was to grow worse before it grew better. No longer young, he remained the plaything of his passions and plunged into a morass when he set eyes on Marta de Nevares Santoyo. This is a repugnant story upon which it would be superfluous to dwell. Meanwhile Lope's pen was as indefatigable as ever. He made a bid for fame in the province of devout history, and in 1618 dedicated to the great historian, Mariana, his account of the martyrs who had perished recently in Japan. This is not one of his happiest efforts, for Lope has not the gift of clearness: he wrote too rapidly to be lucid. But he could not resist the temptation to outshine everybody in every sphere. Cervantes had succeeded greatly with *Don*

Quixote and with the *Novelas exemplares*. This was a sufficient goad to Lope who accordingly intercalated a prose story in *La Filomena* (1621). Dedicated to Marcia Leonardo (a pseudonym for Marta de Nevares Santoyo), it is an undeniable failure. Three more stories introduced into *La Circe* (1624) are not much more successful: as a novelist, Lope was not destined to shine. At the same time, the verses in both the volumes just mentioned are often admirable, though they suffer from the writer's habitual improvising methods. They are, withal, better than his attempt to outdo Petrarch in the *Triunfos divinos* (1625). The *Corona trágica* (1627) is more interesting to English readers than to Spaniards; for here Lope idealizes Mary Stuart and takes for gospel all the admiring remarks on that queen consigned in the life of her by the English Dominican George Conn. Lope was a day behind the fair. It was a little too late to persuade the world that Mary Stuart was a fit subject for canonization.

But that is not the weak point of the *Corona trágica*. It fails because the inspiration is intermittent, because Lope is a poet for five lines and then is dull for ten pages. He is himself again in *La Dorotea* (1632), a sort of autobiography, a kind of prose play in which he introduces much admirable but obscure verse imbedded in rich and curious archaic prose. He had kept this play by his right hand for half a century, and was perpetually retouching it, growing less and less in contact with fact, and more and more inclined to fantastic embellishment. Three years later he issued under the name of Tomé de Burguillos a volume of *Rimas humanas y divinas* which includes *La Gatomachia*, a most brilliant parody of those very Italian epics which he had more than once tried to rival. Lope's last years, or at least months, were troubled. He met for the first time with comparative failure in the theatre, and he was tried by domestic sorrows. His son, Lope Felix, was drowned off Venezuela in 1634; and, as though this were not enough, his favourite daughter fled from home with a gallant. Amid all his sins, follies, and extravagances, Lope had preserved an unshaken faith in the divine ordinance of the universe, and he held the extreme view of most Spaniards as to the inevitability of retribution. He took all his accumulated trials—the death of Marta de Nevares Santoyo after she had lost her sight and gone mad, the loss of Lope Felix at sea, the humiliating flight of Antonia Clara—as punishment for the weaknesses of his past life. To anticipate, or to avert, the wrath of Heaven, the poet locked himself up in his room, and macerated his flesh with *disciplinas* till the walls were splashed with his blood. Meanwhile, his interest in literature, his zeal in poetical composition, continued unabated. On August 23, 1635, he wrote a sonnet and the *silva* entitled *El siglo de oro*; by way of rare distraction he then delved a little in the garden of his house in the Calle de Francos. After the unwonted exertion, he caught a chill, was ordered to keep his

LOPE DE VEGA

bed, and died four days later—on August 27, 1635. Madrid determined to give him a grandiose funeral. People flocked to the procession which went a little out of the direct route, so as to pass before the convent of the Barefooted Trinitarians where Lope's brilliant daughter Marcela was a nun. Lope was buried, as we know, under the high altar in the Church of St. Sebastian in the Calle de Atocha. One might have thought that the passionate pilgrim of eternity had found peace at last, and that he would be disturbed no more. Fate ruled it otherwise. Early in the nineteenth century the Church of St. Sebastian underwent its annual cleaning; a careless workman removed Lope's coffin, and placed it among the rest, without taking the precaution of distinguishing it from them. Hence we can no longer tell precisely where Lope lies; nor are we better informed as regards Cervantes's exact resting-place.

We know rather more about Lope de Vega than we know of any other man of comparable eminence. That eminence he owed chiefly to his dramatic works, and on that point I have purposely said nothing. It is true that if you deprive Lope of his plays, you take half the man away. But the man that is left has done the work of a dozen men. Lope, better than most dramatists, can afford to be despoiled of his immense theatrical capital. If we bear in mind that he was an inexhaustible inventor on the stage, we shall do him no grave injustice in saying that his theatrical achievement, like his achievement in the domain of absolute poetry, is rarely perfect, and is never perfect for any great length of time. If we consider the conditions under which he wrote, we shall be forced to say that it could not be otherwise. He always worked at white heat, under a strain that not one writer in a thousand could long endure. Besieged by impresarios clamouring for new plays, he was bound to improvise lavishly. This was unfortunate for his posthumous fame. He needed the curb, not the spur. Perhaps, I am not sure, he was only too much inclined to rely on his natural fluency, and certainly required no encouragement to rely further on it. Unfortunately this tendency was accentuated by the demands made upon him in the theatres, and this re-acted upon his non-dramatic work. In some of Lope's very weak plays—and some of them are deplorably weak—you will find lines that only a great poet could have written. In some of his best plays there are strange inequalities: confusions of personages, irregularities of metre, sudden changes of metaphor, results of speed or inattention. These defects are noticeable also in much of Lope's non-dramatic work. It sounds plausible to say that Lope de Vega, like the rest of the world, would have done better, had he taken more pains. That may be so. But frankly I am not so certain of it as I should wish to be. Lope spent years upon *La Hermosura de Angélica*, and it is none the more readable for his pains. No: time was not the chief lack from which Lope suffered. What he needed more was a guide in the matter of taste. He had all the Spanish love of the flamboyant, the Spanish desire to impress by sheer voluminousness and bulk. A vast subject tempted him, just as another man's success in a small subject tempted him. And he could resist anything—but temptation. We must candidly admit that, though Lope was far from being a perfect character, we all have a personal weakness for him and are inclined to excuse his follies and to minimize his faults. Indulgence to the man can do no great harm; but we cannot play fast and loose with standards of literary art. Honestly, was Lope a real artist? Yes: at whiles; but not for long. He had no power of selection; he never knew when he had hit the bull's eye, or when he had just grazed the target. By constant writing for the theatre, by laying himself out to please others, he had deadened his artistic conscience. His object was more to satisfy the taste of others than to attain a standard of his own. Lope was a most typical Spaniard and the desire to shine is a most typical Spanish quality. He did not write artistic epics because he was under any innate impulse; he wrote them because others had won fame by writing them. He could have done anything, it seems, if he had not had to do it. But he felt inclined to do everything, and all round he continually falls short of perfection.

We must in common fairness always keep in mind that the national standard of literary taste differs in the North and in the South of Europe. While we produce our best effects by strict attention to detail, the Spaniard produces his by sweeping strokes of a brush overcharged with flaming colour. Lope seeks to dazzle by force rather than by the assiduous elaboration of verbal beauty. He is, in his own way, a master of his instrument; but it is rather a slap-dash way, and one is at last driven to conclude that, great as he often is, he does not quite know all the secrets of instrumentation or, in other words, does not realize all the potentialities of his instrument. Lope is (so to say) a 'sprinter', a short distance runner. An epic is too long for him: he cannot stay the course. On the other hand, he excels in the sonnet, is often most effective in the *romance*, in *quintillas*, or in any other popular form of verse. There are some passages in *Los Pastores de Belen* which for general simplicity and supremacy of execution are matchless. Lope's inequalities are such that he has seldom tempted a translator, and this is a pity, for Lope, as Verstegan recognized, has other beauties besides the second-rate ones which are characteristic of his drama.

LUIS DE GÓNGORA

In most English minds the name of Góngora evokes the image of a man who, without any great flexibility of talent, won a fleeting notoriety by assuming a pose of perverse eccentricity; who flattered popular prejudices, and somehow contrived to infect the literatures of Western Europe by his persistent bad example. This impression is not complete, and—so far as it goes—is not wholly exact. It so happens that Góngora's talent was exceptionally supple; that what is called a 'pose' had with him a basis of intellectual conviction; that instead of flattering the majority, he went out of his way to fight the most deep-rooted tastes of his countrymen and to belittle their most representative spokesman: Lope de Vega. It is often alleged that Góngora corrupted the natural simplicity of literary taste in Spain. Though it is true that his posthumous influence was bad, this sweeping allegation assumes what ought to be proved. Is it a fact that literary taste in Spain tends to simplicity? A long array of instances, extending from Sisebut (or from whoever wrote the letters signed by that far-off king) to Emilio Castelar, might be quoted in favour of the contrary thesis. We must never lose sight of the fact that Spain was long a mere geographical expression, and that, even now, the sense of national unity is not strong, not wide-spread. A man born in this island is an Englishman first of all, a Yorkshireman (say) next. Not so beyond the Pyrenees. Ask your neighbour in the train if he is a Spaniard, and the chances are that he will answer: 'No, sir; I am not a Spaniard; I am a Catalan, or a Galician' as the case may be. It was even so with regard to Góngora. First and foremost, he was a Cordoban. Córdoba was the cradle of Seneca—'him of Cordova dead', as Ben Jonson says—

LUIS DE GÓNGORA

and nobody will maintain that Seneca cultivated unadorned simplicity. When it is said that Góngora infected the literature of Western Europe by force of bad example, the implication is that he was in some direct way responsible for the freaks of Euphuism in England and of Marinism in Italy. Such a notion is pure phantasy, incompatible with the concrete facts of chronology. Let me try to establish that chronology in a rapid survey of the ascertained incidents of Góngora's life, emerging from the darkness which has so long enshrouded it.

Luis de Góngora was born at Córdoba on July 11, 1561. And, before I go any further, I will draw attention to the fact that Góngora was not, strictly speaking, his real name. His father, a petty judge and Inquisitionary official at Córdoba, was called Francisco de Argote; Francisco de Argote married Leonora de Góngora. There is nothing unprecedented in Góngora's assumption of his mother's maiden name: the Spanish practice in such matters was rather loose till the seventeenth century, but there was generally some solid reason for such an act. Góngora's brother took the paternal surname of Argote, and, as everything concerning Luis de Góngora awakens interest, there has been much speculation as to his motive for running counter to custom. We do not know his motive; and there is no ground for the insinuation that he was moved by snobbish reasons. Argote is a name illustrious in Spanish annals, and has a pleasing literary savour about it: as you will remember, the *Conde Lucanor* was first edited (in 1575) by Argote de Molina. But Argote is not a *palabra esdrújula*, a word accented on the antepenultimate. Góngora is such a word, and for words of this kind the poet had an ineradicable weakness duly satirized long afterwards by Tirso de Molina in *La Celosa de sí misma*. Góngora would never say *sepulcro* if he could work in *túmulo*; he cannot bear to write *techo* if *bóveda* is available; *tétrico* means more to him than *triste*, and

LUIS DE GÓNGORA

lóbrego is more expressive than *obscuro*. Had the maiden name of the poet's mother not been a *palabra esdrújula*, probably Argote would be precisely as famous as— no more and no less famous than—the name of Góngora now is. That name owes all its celebrity to him. He might have said, as Alfred de Vigny long afterwards said,

J'ai fait illustre un nom qu'on m'a transmis sans gloire.
Qu'il soit ancien, qu'importe? Il n'aura de mémoire
Que du jour seulement où mon front l'a porté.

If the boy was father of the man, Góngora's motive in assuming his mother's maiden name is easily understood. He was by no means a distinguished undergraduate; he idled his time away, was known as a good dancer and fencer, left Salamanca in 1580 without a degree, and, though much better off than most of his comrades, he had a millstone of debts round his neck. Fortunately, his mother's brother, a prosperous prebendary, came to the rescue. Observe: I have just said that Góngora left Salamanca in 1580. Now the First Part of *Euphues* appeared in 1579. Can anybody in his senses maintain that Lyly, then close on fifty years of age, wrote under the literary influence of a lad of eighteen whom he had never seen, who lived at the other end of Europe, and who had, as yet, never printed a line? It is strange that a theory so absurd should ever have been entertained.

On quitting Salamanca, Góngora took orders. He was a sound churchman, and brought no discredit on his cloth. Still, it would be idle to pretend that he entered the Church from any high motive. He shared the views of his contemporaries on such matters, and those views were as lax as the practice of the time was lax. Many of these contemporaries took orders for utilitarian reasons. Góngora was no exception. While still an undergraduate at Salamanca, he had been 'jobbed' into two or three small livings, and the example of his maternal uncle's success may have weighed with him. At all events in 1585 he obtained a prebendary at Córdoba. It should be observed that he was not yet a priest, and, in fact, fourteen years later — in 1599—he was still only a deacon. We must suppose that he obtained his prebendary through local influence, either that of his father, or mother, or of his uncle.

He apparently found it hard to settle down in his new surroundings. Or, it may be that his rapid preferment awakened jealousies. At any rate, unfavourable rumours began to circulate about him, and in 1589 his bishop appointed a committee to inquire into the truth of them. They really amounted to very little. Góngora was alleged to be irregular in attending divine service, and to be given to talking to his neighbours in church. He was further accused of receiving actors at his house, of being present at bull-fights, and of frequenting company which indulged in personal gossip. Lastly—and this was perhaps thought to be the gravest charge against him—Góngora was said to be in the habit of writing verses on profane, that is secular, subjects. Góngora's replies were not over respectful to his judges, but his solemn flippancy is characteristic. He states that his attendance at divine service was, at least, not more irregular than that of the other members of the chapter; he denies point-blank the charge of talking in church, observing that his neighbour on one side of him is stone-deaf, while the canon in the stall on the other side never stops singing, so that it would be impossible for him to talk, even if he wished to do so. He says that actors had called on him at his house, as they called at the houses of other respectable people in Córdoba; he admits going to bull-fights and frequenting company where some personal gossip went on. But (he adds slyly) both at the bull-fights and in the gossiping circles, he met with a good number of clerics of senior standing to his own. Góngora is much more serious in dealing with the charge of writing secular verses. He cannot indeed deny it altogether, for he was known to write poems, and had already been publicly complimented in print as a 'matchless genius' by Cervantes in the *Galatea* (1585). What Góngora states is that these stories about his versifying propensities are overdone; that many copies of verses which were circulated over his name were not by him at all, and that, if he did not write on devotional subjects that was because he felt himself insufficiently equipped for theological flights. It is better, he ends dryly, to be accused of frivolity than to be burnt for heresy.

Since Góngora hints that he was not responsible for all the verses circulated with his name attached to them, there is no more to be said on that head, except that some authentic verses of his might be objected to by persons not over prudish. Anyhow, his explanations were accepted by his ecclesiastical superiors, and the charges against him did him no harm. The Chapter of Córdoba entrusted him with several important missions which led him to visit remote parts of Spain: traces of these professional journeys are noticeable in many of his poems which bespeak a minute observation of nature not very common among contemporary Spanish poets. Though he fell seriously ill in 1593, and was henceforth somewhat less active physically, his intellectual powers grew rather than diminished. In 1605 he contributed lavishly to Pedro Espinosa's *Flores de poetas ilustres de España*, and this anthology, though not a popular success, made Góngora's name familiar to genuine lovers of poetry in Spain. Some four years later his health failed; he suffered from intense and continuous headaches; at the same time his writing underwent a radical modification. Spain being what it is, the rumour went about that Góngora's mind was affected. There is no foundation for this cruel and malignant assertion. It is refuted by the fact that he was appointed Treasurer of the Chapter at Córdoba in 1610. If he had gone out of his mind in 1609, is it at all likely that his colleagues who saw him every day, would entrust him with the administration of their funds? Spaniards are anything but confiding and careless in money matters. The whole story is frankly incredible, one of many calumnies against Góngora. Possibly some inkling of these slanders reached him, and induced him to leave Córdoba. In 1612 he removed to Madrid. Somehow or other, he had scraped acquaintance with the Duke of Lerma, and, through the influence of that Prime Minister, he was appointed chaplain to Philip III. Clearly he must have been ordained priest in or before 1612. However, the post was purely honorary. Lerma fell from power before he could do any more for Góngora, and though the poet remained twelve years at the capital, he was constantly in painful financial distress. Some letters of his, written at this period, are depressing reading, so packed are they with afflicting details of want, and even penury. After a spell of time spent at Córdoba, Góngora returned to Court, accompanied Philip IV to Aragón, fell seriously ill, and hurried back to Córdoba, where he lingered a year, having lost his memory. He died at Córdoba on May 23, 1627, in the little white house in the Plazuela de la Trinidad to which every literary pilgrim pays (or should pay) a visit after seeing the Mezquita.

Góngora, as we have seen, was not above mixing with actors, and—living when he did—he would not have been a typical Spaniard, had he not tried his hand as a playwright. One might have guessed that his wit, his grace, his fine irony would have made an effect in the theatre. One would have been quite wrong. We know that he failed as a dramatist, and the only complete piece of his which survives, *Las Firmezas de Isabel*, exhibits him at his weakest. Clearly he had no great natural vocation for what Azorín calls 'the most commercial form of literary art'. We may perhaps assume

LUIS DE GÓNGORA

that *Las Firmezas de Isabel*—as well as the fragmentary *Comedia Venatoria* and the incomplete *Doctor Carlino*—were written as mere 'potboilers', without much hope of success. Absolute poetry claimed Góngora for her own. Poetry absorbed all his powers, and, to such effect, that he is the typical Spanish poet of the seventeenth century as Garci Lasso is the typical Spanish poet of the sixteenth century. For Garci Lasso's nymphs and fawns and glades and waterfalls Góngora substituted a more subtle note of Puck-like irony. There exists a portrait of him ascribed (perhaps wrongly) to Velazquez; painted in his later days, it reveals him as an arrogant pontiff, dominating all within range. This is not the youthful Góngora of the *letrillas* and *romances* which constitute his real title to admiration. In these compositions he manifests an impertinent wit, a sunny gaiety, a pardonable, sparkling insolence full of youthful charm. The immaturity of the writer is evident; in every line we find a bold personal touch, a quaint, bantering, piquant fancy. He writes as a young man will, imitatively keeping within the limits of the national tradition. We catch echoes of the classics, of Petrarch, of the two Tassos, and of Ariosto; among Spaniards, none influences his early expression more than his fellow-Andalusian, Fernando de Herrera, with his southern pomp, altisonant rhetoric and dulcet melody. But this is only a passing phase. Like Herrera, his adoration of Garci Lasso is complete. Like Herrera, he is shocked at Boscan's defective craftsmanship and crabbed numbers. In this respect, he was unrepentant. In his version of the story of Hero and Leander, he glances at Boscan's *Leandro*, the first attempt at blank verse in Spanish. Góngora's reference is unkind.

For my part, let my word be frank.
I'd count it one of Heaven's greater mercies
To meet a wild bull loose, point blank,
Than one of Boscan's loose blank verses.

The point of the jest lies in the play upon

words *buey suelto* and *versos sueltos*. In his ode to the Armada,

'*Levanta, España, tu famosa diestra*'

Góngora chiefly models himself on Herrera's celebrated *Song of Lepanto*. But already he is a better executant than his master. His pre-occupation with form is unmistakable, and from that he never departed.

Cervantes's allusion to him proves that Góngora was early recognized as a brilliant versifier. But to be praised with a crowd of nonentities did not content Góngora. He aspired to something more than local fame, and perhaps expected to win this when contributing to Espinosa's *Flores de poetas ilustres de España*. If so, he was disappointed. The most popular poet of the day was Lope de Vega, a gifted but careless workman whose abounding exuberance captured the general public. Góngora recognized that he could not vie with Lope in volume and facility. He determined to appeal to the learned, the exquisite, the refined, the cultured (*los cultos*). Hence the word *culteranismo*, an expression invented apparently by Ximenez Paton, often used as a synonym for what we call Gongorism, and for what at the outset was called the *nueva poesía*.

Whatever may have been Góngora's reasons for changing his style, there is no denying that his last manner differs profoundly from that of his first or middle periods. First of all, he is satirical and derivative with a tendency to copy Herrera's flamboyant epithets and plangent music. Next, Góngora 'finds himself', and is incomparably dainty, observant, sub-acid, adroit—and this is the best Góngora. Finally, there is the Góngora who is identified with Gongorism—revelling in verbal obscurities, in enigmatic metaphors, in emphatic hyperbaton, in crude antithesis, and in open revolt against conventional syntax. When did he take the plunge? Was the innovation a wholly original idea of his own, or did he develop hints discoverable elsewhere?

It used to be thought that he received the first impulse from Marino's *Adone*. But is this possible? Consider a moment: the *Adone* was not published till 1623, and Góngora died in 1627, having changed his manner some seventeen or eighteen years previously. The first unmistakable signs of his new evolution are noticeable in his eulogy on Lerma: this composition was written in 1609 and is undeniably a new departure. The poem on the capture of Larache dates from 1610, and here the symptoms are, if anything, more pronounced. It cannot be maintained that we are faced with the chance caprice of an experimenter. No: we are confronted with a deliberate policy —with a system which was further developed till it culminated in the tortuous perplexities of the *Polifemo y Galatea* and the impenetrable mysteries of the *Soledades* —which few, even of the elect, have ever pretended to understand thoroughly. In these two poems we have *culteranismo* raised to its highest power: according to some, they are the abomination of desolation; according to others, they are the climax of poetic sublimity.

Now, poetical systems do not come into existence complete, as Minerva sprang from the brain of Jove. Góngora long afterwards averred that he had been set on the new track by one much younger than himself, a marvellous genius whom he did not identify more precisely. This gifted being was a young soldier, Luis Carrillo y Sotomayor who was also a native of Córdoba, and who died prematurely in 1611, leaving behind him a volume entitled *Obras*, published in 1610. It is quite clear that there are similarities between Góngora's *Polifemo y Galatea* and Carrillo's poem, the *Fábula de Atis y Galatea*. But these similarities might be accidental, due to a certain likeness of subject, or they might even be due to unconscious reminiscence. However, it was not from Carrillo's poems that Góngora got his idea. That came from a prose document—*Libro de la Erudición*

LUIS DE GÓNGORA

poética—at the end of Carrillo's *Obras*. This is a sort of literary manifesto, written not later than 1607, circulated in manuscript long before it was printed and much discussed in literary circles before it was given to the public. The document, far too long to quote, while it deprecates too dense an obscurity, suggests that lucidity in a poem is rather a blemish than a merit. Góngora 'found salvation' on the spot and put this theory into practice in his *Panegyrico al duque de Lerma* in 1609. He had incomparably more genius than Carrillo, more combativeness, more strength, more obstinacy (if we may use that disagreeable word). He had vastly more logic and carried out the new theories with radical consistency. However, he did not assume that he would win the day without a struggle, and before going to extremities he bethought him of an ally, a possible ally. By 1613 he had written his incomprehensible *Polifemo* and his not less incomprehensible *Soledades*. He determined to submit both to the judgement of his friend Pedro de Valencia, then the foremost scholar of Spain. It was an astute plan. If Valencia proved hostile, Góngora would be no worse off than before. If Valencia were favourable, his authority would impress the average man who (it might be) was not aware that Valencia and Góngora were on intimate terms. Yes: Valencia was on good terms with Góngora, but he could be trusted to deal faithfully with a friend. His verdict was not reassuring. Though he employed all manner of polite formulae and ingratiating phrases, he censured what he called the *cacosyntheton* and the *cacozelia* of both poems, denounced the innovations *en bloc*, and ended on a friendly note with some criticisms of detail. Góngora condescended to accept some of the minor suggestions. But he could only do so to a limited extent. Many manuscript copies of the first drafts were already in existence, and could not be recalled. The original readings held the field. We must not forget that Góngora's later works were not printed in his lifetime, and that his immense reputation was, so to say, a manuscript reputation. In our own day, on a smaller scale, something of the same sort has occurred in the cases of D. G. Rossetti and of the French poet José-Maria de Heredia, though both of these did live to see their poems in print.

Góngora, shy, proud, and reserved, courted no publicity. His appeal was esoteric; the only applause which he sought was that of the chosen few. He obtained it by slow degrees, and the crowd followed like sheep—followed in numbers which made established favourites uneasy. We know that Tennyson was not a little perturbed at one time by the increasing vogue of Swinburne and Morris. It was not unnatural. Nobody likes to think that his day is over, that he is a 'fogy', as Sir Barnes Lawrence disrespectfully said of his uncle. Just so, Lope de Vega who always had his finger on the public pulse. was concerned to observe that the younger men were rallying to Góngora. Enough of the Old School remained to indulge in bitter criticism. Góngora took no part in formal public polemics; if some spiteful remark floated up to him, he took his revenge by relapsing into his earlier manner and penning a caustic epigram or stinging sonnet which everybody—especially the victim—could understand without difficulty. It was evident that his right hand had not lost its cunning and that he was a most formidable foe. His contemptuous silence in public embarrassed his antagonists and filled them with a sort of terror. Even Lope de Vega found it expedient to pay court to Góngora in private, but Góngora set too just a value on himself to be beguiled by courteous phrases or amiable attentions. He knew that his partisans were increasing in numbers, knew that his natural opponents were divided among themselves. It is true that Lope de Vega was a declared opponent of the new methods and of the new poetry generally. But, if Lope were known to be on one side, you might feel pretty sure that Cervantes would be on the other. So it proved in this case. In the *Viage del Parnaso* Cervantes went out of his way to pay a compliment to the 'Polyphemean stanzas' of Góngora. Possibly enough Cervantes did not succeed any better than most of the human race in understanding *Polyfemo y Galatea*. But a compliment is always a compliment, and, though his influence in Spain was much less than Lope's, his name carried a certain weight, especially north of the Pyrenees.

One immense difficulty in the way of forming a critical estimate of Góngora's poems was removed in 1921 by M. Foulché-Delbosc's edition in the Bibliotheca Hispanica (6). Until then no good edition of Góngora existed. Góngora's dislike of publicity, though creditable to him as a man, was a posthumous artistic hindrance. Every now and then, when he felt the pinch of poverty, he toyed with the notion of publishing his poems, but he ended by doing nothing. Another obstacle in the way of forming a good edition of Góngora's verses lay in the fact that he could never leave anything alone, that he had a passion for revising every scrap that he had written. There is in the Biblioteca Nacional at Madrid a very splendid manuscript copy of Góngora's verses collected during eight years by Antonio Chacon Ponce de Leon who proposed to dedicate the work to the omnipotent Prime Minister Olivares. Chacon Ponce de Leon alleges—and I see no reason to doubt him—that this manuscript was revised by Góngora who added the dates of composition in each case throughout. It is on this manuscript that the edition of Góngora's poems in the Bibliotheca Hispanica is based. The main defect of the Chacon Ponce de Leon manuscript is the omission in it of Góngora's satirical poems. This has been taken into account by M. Foulché-Delbosc, as may be seen by the third volume of his edition. Góngora was never more brilliant, more characteristic than in his mordant vein. As he grew older he regretted his youthful impetuosity and, as has been already said, suppressed all compositions of a personal character. Though this no doubt does credit to his placable temper, it cannot be approved by any editor. Moreover it is highly misleading and gives a very incomplete, not to say wrong, impression of the writer's career. Leave the satirical element out of Góngora and you have bisected Góngora at the waist. It is Samson with his hair cut. And, as if this were not enough, Góngora's mania for revision is a perpetual and perhaps insuperable stumbling-block. But no critical considerations of this kind deterred those who had known him. Editions were hurried out soon after he died. The first edition in the field was that of Juan Lopez de Vicuña who was not lacking in courage, though deficient in humour. Within a year of Góngora's death, Lopez de Vicuña brought out an edition on the title-page of which he described Góngora as 'the Spanish Homer'. Nothing could well be more inept, for Góngora was not the least like Homer; but, at the moment, it would have been thought indecent or sacrilegious to make so pedantic a point. The phrase was well understood to be a formal flourish, a polite arabesque, not erring in the direction of hyperbole. Just then, many would have been prepared (without having read either poet) to maintain that Góngora was far greater than Homer. Other editions followed in rapid succession, each edition finding fault with its predecessors. We can readily agree with the hard things which most of the editors said of one another. Yet we ought to hesitate before blaming them, for they had a most difficult task. By his reticence, no less than by his obscurity, his persistent mania for emendation, retouching and recasting, Góngora has set all editors an almost insoluble problem. His indifference or good nature in allowing all manner of incompetents to copy his poems, his lavishness in giving away his own manuscripts to anybody who asked for them are equally sources of error and causes of recrimination. Not only were there gaps in the current editions. Worse than that: the current editions contained poems for which Góngora has no responsibility whatever. Some of these are poor things: others are not unworthy of him. He is often credited with a charming poem: '*Mil años ha que no canto*'. It is far more likely to be by Lope de Vega who, though against Gongorism in theory, was far too astute, and far too susceptible to every surrounding influence, not to 'drop into' (as Mr. Wegg would say) Gongorism in practice. Then there is a delightful *romance*: *Así Riselo cantaba*. This poem is almost certainly not by Góngora, though it appears among his works. There is some reason to think that it may be ascribed to Pedro Liñan de Riaza, a minor poet who predeceased Góngora by some twenty years, and never wrote anything else nearly so good. But, after all, this is not established fact, and, as we do not really know for certain who wrote *Así Riselo cantaba*, it must be described as being by an anonymous author.

Francisco Cascales, a contemporary, declared that there were two Góngoras, one an angel of light and the other an angel of darkness. This estimate is, roughly speaking, sound. There are passages in some of his later writings which are staggering in their unintelligibility. It is not given to all of us to strike an attitude of reverential admiration before what we cannot understand, like Pellicer, who observes in one of his elucidatory notes: 'This is what I have contrived to guess at in explaining passages so difficult as those of Góngora in his *Soledades*: my intelligence can do no more.' Some of us may regret that the commentator's intelligence did so much. Many of these gentry only serve to make the darkness of the text still denser. But, if Góngora is obscure at his worst—

LUIS DE GÓNGORA

and he is not so obscure as his imitators—he is inimitable at his best. Take, for instance, the *romance* beginning '*Las flores del romero*', the airy grace and ingenious fancy of whose charming lines have been well reproduced by Archdeacon Churton (7) under the title of *The Rosemary Spray*.

The flowers upon the rosemary spray,
Young Maid, may school thy sorrow;
The blue-eyed flower, that blooms to-day,
To honey turns to-morrow.

A tumult stirs thy tender breast.
With jealous pain true-hearted,
That he, whom thy first love hath bless'd
From thee hath coldly parted.

Ungracious boy, who slights thy love,
And overbold, disdaining
To ask forgiveness, and remove
The cause of thy complaining.

Hope, come and drive those tears away!
For lovers' jealous sorrow,
Like dewy blue-eyed flower on spray
To honey turns to-morrow.

By thine own joy thou wast undone:
A bliss thou couldst not measure,
Like star at dawn too near the sun,
Eclipsed thee by its pleasure.

Walk forth with eyes serene and fair;
The pearls, that deck the morning,
Are wasted in the day's fierce glare;
With calmness tame his scorning.

Disperse those clouds that but dismay;
Distrust that jealous sorrow:
The blue-eyed flower, that blooms to-day,
To honey turns to-morrow.

These are verses which any poet might have been proud to write. That Góngora is one of the greatest names in Spanish literature is now universally admitted. It was not always so, for I remember in my salad days that one was looked at askance for expressing some such view. Spaniards winced at being reminded that Cervantes and Lope de Vega agreed, however much they differed from Góngora, in lauding his wonderful powers: for Cervantes, as we have seen, Góngora was a 'matchless genius'; for Lope he was 'the rarest wit ever produced by his native province.' That Góngora was an innovator is true. It is also true that many of his innovations were ill-advised and have been rejected by posterity. But we must not judge him as if he had written nothing but the *Polifemo* and the *Soledades*. And though I am no admirer of these poems, I am bound to confess that most of us critics, historians, and the like have scarcely treated them with complete fairness. Even the judicial Ticknor scoffs at Góngora because in the *Soledades* he describes a village bride as being 'so beautiful that she might parch Norway with her two suns, and bleach Ethiopia with her two hands.' No doubt, if you translate verse into prose, and studiously select the most pedestrian style for your rendering, you can produce a ludicrous effect. But that is not translation at all: it is grotesque parody. What Góngora says is this:

> Her twin-born sunbright eyes
> Might turn to summer Norway's wintry skies;
> And the white wonder of her snowy hand
> Blanch with surprise the sons of Ethiopian land.

It may not appeal to your taste; but as a deliberate exercise in hyperbole there is nothing intolerable about it.

Góngora was an innovator, but he was not a revolutionary. He did not, so far as I have observed, attempt to introduce any new poetic form as his butt, Boscan, had done half a century earlier. He would have contended that his aims and methods were more modest and more prudent. He sought to rejuvenate the poetic diction of Spain, to enrich the current vocabulary, to eschew the trite phrase, to extirpate the banal conventional epithet, to impart a new flexibility to an unwieldy syntax, to substitute distinction for a cheap facility. No ambition could be more thoroughly justifiable. It is less easy to vindicate Góngora's execution: it is not always on a level with the design. What is intended to be impressive and euphonious is often pompous and metallic. That is so with Góngora himself in the *Polifemo* and the *Soledades*: the pomposity and brassiness are, of course, more marked in the disciples than in the master. The disciples had little but mannerisms at their command: the master could summon his genius—his prompt and scintillating genius—at will. And that summons was often issued. Góngora was betrayed by too close an adherence to aesthetic principles which were not his own. He appears at moments to lose faith in Carrillo's theories, and becomes himself once more. Some of his later *letrillas* are among the most brilliant of his efforts, and they flash with blinding splendour, amid the general atmosphere of 'inspissated gloom.' At such instants—and there are many of them—it is plain that Góngora has abjured Gongorism. He survives by virtue of his shimmering fancy, his bitter-sweet irony, his frosty clarity. And his conscientious workmanship assures his survival also as a sound literary influence. No doubt he counts for something in the labyrinthine obscurities of such a writer as Ros de Olano. He reacts also on writers to whom his name is anathema : he counts for a great deal in the general attitude, the lancinating grace, the insinuating finish of Juan Valera (who, like him, by the way, was born in the province of Córdoba). Speaking broadly, Spaniards have not been much pre-occupied in solving problems of stylistic perfection. But if it is now admitted that such problems exist, and if in each generation a few writers seek for practical solutions, they are marching under Góngora's standard. Whether they admit it or not, all Spanish writers interested in form are his debtors.

SOME LATER POETS

Soon after the battle of Rocroi, the long-impending collapse of Spain took place. When it occurred, it was complete. Art and literature seemed to vanish on the day that Condé broke the famous *tercios* of Spanish infantry on the Flemish frontier. A few eminent figures flitted past on the literary scene, but they are rather the embarrassed phantoms of departed splendour and dead traditions than intellectual vital forces. The great Calderon himself, who lived till 1681, cannot be ranked as an independent initiator; he develops with subtle skill the germs of Lope's work. And roughly—for practical purposes—we may consider Calderon as the noblest representative of the seventeenth century, through the greater part of which he lived. So far as literature is concerned, the eighteenth century, a time of ferment elsewhere, is even worse than the end of the seventeenth century.

A fair case might be made for refusing to grant Diego Tadeo Gonzalez (who was born more than half a century after Calderon died) the title of a poet at all. Still, he had the accomplishment of verse, and, in a happy moment, he—writing rather above his ordinary form—produced *El murciélago alevoso* which even the most grudging anthologist is compelled to admit. A loftier spirit is that of the elder Moratin, and a statelier figure is that of Jovellanos; but Moratin's experiences on the stage damped his poetic fire, and as to Jovellanos, he, like Burke, 'to party gave up what was meant for mankind'. It is as difficult to do justice to Melendez Valdés, a man of no character, unstable as a weather-cock in a hurricane; his excellent technique does not compensate for the insincerity which mars nearly all his work.

It took the French Revolution and the legions of Napoleon to rouse Spain from her lethargy. The invaders learned that

SOME LATER POETS

Spain, like Juliet, was not dead but sleeping. A few leaders found thousands ready to follow them, ready to die for principles which seemed to have been extinguished since the time that Charles V crushed Pedro Lasso de la Vega and the *Comuneros*. The energy of the masses reacted upon the educated class. Men like Quintana and Gallego chanted the prowess of their embattled countrymen and denounced the tyranny of the foreign oppressor. Napoleon failed to destroy Spain: incidentally, he brought Spanish poetry to life again. Still more was unwittingly done in this direction by the wretched Fernando Séptimo, one of the worst kings in history. Restored to the throne amid the acclamations of an adoring, credulous, patriotic people, Fernando soon contrived to band all independent men against him, and before ten years were out many of these men were driven into exile. What followed might have been foreseen. An amnesty had to be declared, and the exiles returned imbued with foreign ideals. Romanticism in literature was the counterpart of their political theories. Some, like the Duque de Rivas, tried to make the best of both worlds. Under the guidance of John Hookham Frere, an ex-ambassador at Madrid and the first man to suggest an emendation in the text of the *Poema del Cid*, Rivas became a Romantic poet. On the stage he soon became the head of the Romantic movement and by sheer merit, originality and force, took the place which Martinez de la Rosa had momentarily occupied. The piece which made his reputation on the boards was *Don Álvaro o La Fuerza del Sino* : this was first given on March 22, 1835, a date to be remembered, for a whole legend is attached to the *estreno* of *Don Álvaro* as a whole legend has crystallized round the first production of *Hernani*. *Hernani* preserves something of its ancient potency. Hardened playgoers admit that they are not unmoved still when they hear the horn blow. *Don Álvaro* has not the same gift of eternal youth : it no longer stirs and moves us: but it served its purpose that March night, eighty-eight years ago. It is doubtful whether Rivas would have won enduring fame as a poet, even had be been content to exchange for that possibility the ephemeral repute of a Cabinet Minister.

Not all the returned exiles were so complacent. The most brilliant figure amongst them, José de Espronceda, modelled his private life too closely upon that of Byron, and, however vehemently the fact may be denied by excitable biographers, it is certain that passages of Espronceda's are redolent of Byron. Some years ago there were people in England who rather doubted if Byron deserved to be classified as a poet at all. To foreigners these doubts, scruples, and hesitations have not occurred. Incapable of perceiving his defective craftsmanship, they regard Byron as one of the great elemental literary forces in the world. That was Espronceda's view: a view shared by all the Romance races from Venice to Lima. We need not share it, but we may do well to bear in mind the familiar saying that foreign opinion is apt to be an anticipation of the verdict of posterity. Espronceda's affinities with Byron have rather told against him in Spain where critics are unaware that there is nothing in Byron so roving, so impassioned, and so sincere as the famous *Canto a Teresa*. But the reaction in Spain against Espronceda, which happened unluckily to reach its highest point just about the time of his first centenary, is a by-product of excessive nationalism, and is in great part due to a desire to exalt José Zorrilla. The difference between the two is not unlike the difference between an eagle and a flamingo: the flamingo is gay in colouring, but his flight is on a lower plane. Zorrilla has all the qualities which Spaniards are wont to prize: brilliancy, gorgeous epithet, an inexhaustible fluency. Yes! he has all these gifts. But Zorrilla has one defect, and that happens to be fatal. He is verbose, and yet has nothing, or hardly anything to say.

So far, we have been concerned with men of the past. I am not unaware that some of us might have seen Zorrilla who died only thirty years ago. But his influence had ceased long before his death, and counted for nothing vital in Spanish literature. His best work was done long before 1855 when he went to Mexico where he remained for nearly a dozen years. On his return to Spain he found that his popularity had fled, and that the favourite of the day was a contemporary of his own, who long outlived him. This was Ramon de Campoamor y Campoosorio. Campoamor, in his old age, was one of the sights of Madrid. Nobody would have guessed that the spruce, fastidious, sharp-tongued, peppery, cynical old gentleman who held a *levée* in Fernando Fe's bookshop had started in life as a tumultuous, dishevelled romantic poet. Campoamor had made a false start but, being in many respects the incarnation of commonsense, he recognized the absurdity (in him) of the 'romantic' pose, perceived also that the days of Romanticism were numbered, left it in the lurch, and, after one or two bids for fame on the stage, reappeared as a poet with a subdued manner of his own. It cannot be said that he was a very sublime poet: he did not aim at sublimity, but he was a most adroit versifier, an accomplished master of his art: moreover, he had an extensive knowledge of the world; he had wit, grace, charm, ingenuity, fancy, and a sympathy with human emotion which was perhaps rather deeper than he was willing to show. There is very little observation of nature or still-life in Campoamor: landscape interests him solely as the necessary background to his favourite types of humanity: his instinctive, emotional woman—the incarnation of the Eternal Feminine!—and his satiated, disillusioned man—the symbol of the Everlasting Male! There is a constant tart flavour in Campoamor: there is no corrosive bitterness in him. To Campoamor life was rather a sparkling comedy of errors than a panorama of tragic situations. But it is an exaggeration to say that he took nothing seriously, and that he sought refuge from realities in a mocking scepticism. The mockery and the scepticism are nearly always there, but every now and then he allows us to see that his gay incredulity is interpenetrated with a gravity based on insight. This is visible enough for example in the *humorada* beginning '*Vi una cruz en despoblado . . .*' This *humorada* is typical in its conciseness and in its sentiment: and its brevity, as well as its characteristic quality, encourages me to attempt a rough rendering:

One day a cross came into view,
   When I had crossed a desert plain,
And one I chanced to meet said—'There
   A soldier had a bandit slain.'

But . . . oh! tradition's perfidy!
   As I was turning home again
A second man informed me—'There
   A bandit had a soldier slain.'

Though not great poetry, this *humorada* contains an idea, is (in the original Spanish) ingeniously phrased, and is not lacking in malicious subtlety. One can readily understand that countless compositions of this sort, distinguished for the excellence of their technique, for their adroit avoidance of repetition, would ensure their author an extensive popularity.

And, as it chanced, Campoamor was in a position to promote his popularity. Though not a millionaire, he was independent of publishers; he did not, so it appears, trouble to copyright anything that came from his pen; any publisher anywhere was free to reproduce whatever he chose of Campoamor's. He was a goldmine to enterprising traders in books. Editions of his works were innumerable and cheap; every speculating bookseller was personally interested in 'pushing' the sale of those wares; and finally, it was almost impossible to find anybody who had not read ¡ Quien supiera escribir !

Campoamor's vogue in and out of Spain was never seriously threatened, but there were at least two other writers who deserved to be considered as rivals, and who for a time seemed likely to supplant him. One of these was Gustavo Adolfo Bécquer, doubtless of German extraction, to judge by his name. Bécquer was a Bohemian by temperament, and was not likely to be seen in the social circles of which Campoamor was the ornament. The poor soul was more accustomed to lodgings at the sign of *la belle étoile* than to frequenting fashionable drawing-rooms. But he undeniably brought something new into Spanish literature, substituted a dreamy atmosphere of elfin enchantment for the intense lucidity of Spanish verse, and, though he professed to be unable to read German, shows unmistakable signs of affiliation with Heine. He has not Heine's penetrating irony nor his seductive charm; nor has he Heine's certainty of touch; his ear is apt to be defective, and his vagueness makes him seem elusive. But he has happy moments, and in the art of suggestion he has no rival in his own domain. Nor shall we find one in any kindred art till much later—in the person of Debussy. Bécquer's melancholy numbers, monotonous and apparently artless as cradle-songs, made him (especially after his death when his poems were first collected) a favourite with women.

A poet who struck a more virile note which attracted men, especially political men, in a very high degree was Gaspar Núñez de Arce. I speak of Núñez de Arce with some reserve, as he was an intimate personal friend of mine. Before I go any further let me remark upon the date of his birth, as given in the *Oxford Book of Spanish Verse*. It is the date which is given in all the books of reference, but Núñez de Arce appears to have been doubtful on the point himself and gradually acquired the conviction that he was a year or two older. There seems to have been some informality in the register at Valladolid where he was born, and the probability is that 1834 should read 1832. Núñez de Arce came into note first of all as a precocious dramatist, and he long continued to tempt fortune on the stage.

Then he strayed into the political labyrinth, and, strange to say, lost nothing by it, except his ease and peace of mind. He could have called himself a democrat, and no doubt his convictions were of that type. But he lived in troubled times; and, as it happened, his companions were men of a more exaggerated logic than himself. It is not my business to discuss the events which occurred in Spain after the downfall of the Bourbon Dynasty. The disappearance of Isabel II was no doubt hailed with satisfaction by Núñez de Arce, as by most honest Spaniards of the day. They and he were disappointed by the result. Núñez de Arce had the gift of vision: he had not the gift of prevision. Fundamentally he was an optimist, but the experiences which he went through in the years immediately following 1870 left an abiding mark upon him. He was appalled at the anarchy of the streets, of the administration, of the Cortes, of the army, of the navy, of the civil population. 'It had never occurred to me', he remarked once, 'that liberty would be interpreted to mean stealing your neighbour's watch and cutting your neighbour's throat with impunity.' The optimist was not embittered but discouraged, and in 1875 he launched his famous *Gritos del Combate*, woke up, and found himself notorious. Under the stress of circumstance, the second-rate politician was transformed—so people thought or, at least, said—into a first-class poet. Núñez de Arce was an undoubted poet : whether he was a first-class poet is another matter. Frankly, *Gritos del Combate* is not, in my opinion, his best work, but it is the work by which he is best known, and it won him a triumph which he never repeated. The opportuneness of the book counted for much in its success. To his intense surprise, Núñez de Arce found himself the hero of the Royalist party : he had been perfectly sincere in the *Gritos del Combate*, and could never understand that this volume of verse was exploited by political opponents on the principle that any stick is good enough to beat a dog with—the dog being the Republic which had not materialized into anything like the splendour of his youthful dream. Perhaps Núñez de Arce was meant by nature to chant the praises of ordered liberty. But Spain in his time knew no peace, and even when the Civil War was over, occasion did not favour him. He made the best of it, and turned to less burning themes than were his burden in *Gritos del Combate*. He never failed: his workmanship was too perfect for that. An enemy might ascribe to him the remark which Tennyson is said to have made to a former Master of Trinity : ' I can execute like Shakespeare, but—I have nothing to say '. It would be untrue, no doubt, an incomplete statement of the case, as regards both men. Núñez de Arce is a representative of his time. The hopes, fears, and doubts of his generation become articulate in him. And he has a fine sympathy with nature and with human emotions. What he thinks of Byron, how he portrays Luther, these are now matters of secondary interest. But there is an abiding interest in his handling of the simpler aspects of life in *La Pesca*, or in his treatment of a boy's love for a girl in his *Idilio*. In the latter poem he seems to me to reach his highest point of excellence, and he narrates with such effect that a critical, unsentimental reader, reading the poem professionally for the press has been known to end in a passion of tears. If the fates were cruel in denying to Núñez de Arce the opportunity, for which he longed, to repeat his exploit in the domain of lyric patriotism, they made amends by bestowing upon him other compensatory gifts with a prodigal hand. This was not his own view of the matter. He was not resigned to the decrees of destiny. He felt that he could have been other—and greater – than he was. Public disasters oppressed him. His health broke down. His political career was not a success. The optimism of his youth gave way to a depressing pessimism. He ceased to have a mind open to new ideas, and even in the domain of art he was unable to assimilate the new theories of poetical technique which were in the air. He himself was a convinced Parnassian and when Parnassianism was threatened, he felt that the end of the world was at hand. There had been a time when he could boast of founding a school which included men like Emilio Ferrari and Manuel Reina, but that time was past, and it afflicted Núñez de Arce unspeakably to find that Reina was susceptible to new influences which he himself could not feel.

These influences had long been in the air, but they gathered their chief momentum from Spanish-America. Spanish-America was in the way to form an independent poetic literature of her own. In far-off days, before Spanish-America had attained political independence, South America had been content to follow with docility the literary fashions set by Spain. The Nun of Mexico [Sor Juana Inés de la Cruz] was clearly a Gongorist of the straitest sect. Coming down to more modern days, there is nothing distinctively independent in the work of Andrés Bello and of Olmedo. Heredia is (so to say) an adumbration of Espronceda. The most we can claim for these writers is that their scenery is American. Their mode of feeling, their phrasing, their ideals are eminently Spanish. The Spanish-Americans who came to Madrid either returned (like Felipe Pardo) to be centres of authentic Spanish influence in South America, or if—like Ventura de la Vega, the Avellaneda, or Rafael María Baralt—they settled in Spain, they became hispaniolized, and may be accounted as forming part and parcel of the intellectual wealth of Spain. Perhaps the only South American writer before 1870 whom one could not take for a Spaniard is Gregorio Gutiérrez González, the author of the remarkable *Memoria sobre el cultivo del maíz* (1866), and in his case it is not so much a difference of method as a peculiarity of subject which would set one on one's guard. But at a later date the individuality of South American poets asserts itself more and more emphatically. The accuracy of this statement is not affected by the assertion that some of the tendencies of modern Spanish poetry are first adumbrated in the Castilian verses of a lady whom we all call Rosalía de Castro, but whose legal style was Rosalía Castro de Murguía. When I speak of her 'Castilian verses', it is not otiose padding: for the Señora Murguía was a Galician, wrote verses in Galician to begin with, and was drawing near the end of her life when she produced a volume of verses in Castilian: *En las orillas del Sar.* It is the fashion nowadays to see in this volume the germs of the whole 'modernist' movement in Spanish poetry: but not much importance was attached to it when it appeared in 1884. The book was either neglected altogether, or was considered an interesting if not very successful effort on the part of a bilingual writer to transplant to Castile the 'Celtic magic', a melancholy glamour, of the Galician imagination. It may be that what are now regarded as vital experiments to modify the petrified structure of Spanish verse were explained by the Philistines of 1884 as so many blemishes due to an imperfect mastery of the Castilian instrument.

Not till later, and in another direction, did the reforming impulse take definite form. Everybody knows that modern Spanish literature is much influenced—is too much influenced—by the literary modes that happen to prevail in France at any given moment. No doubt: but what everybody does not say is that no great love is lost between the two races on the opposite sides of the Pyrenees. There is an inexplicable reluctance on the part of Spaniards to admit their literary debt to France—as though all the world were not indebted to France! Campoamor himself was curiously coy in admitting that he had borrowed an idea from Victor Hugo, as though the greatest writers did not borrow lavishly! In the fullness of time the *Symbolistes* won in France:

they could get no hearing in Spain: chiefly because it was impossible to disprove the fact that their theories emanated from France. There was not the same objection to accepting these theories through an intermediary, and, as it happened, two young Spanish-Americans were the pioneers of a poetic revolution which has swept all before it in Spain during the last twenty years or so.

Though not the more potent in influence, the more original temperament of these two youths was that of the Colombian poet José Asunción Silva whose works have been well edited by Señor Sanín Cano. Silva's life was too short to enable him to display all that was in him. He ended it by his own act, before he was thirty-two. All manner of fantastic legends have been put into circulation about him. We have it on the best authority that there is no basis for any of these, I fear I must call them, malignant inventions. A man as successful as Silva is bound to have many enemies. The Spanish-speaking race is not more exempt from envy than the rest of us. The real facts appear to be almost banal in their simplicity. Silva lost his father, and his sister soon afterwards: from the former he inherited a burden of debts which, as a point of honour, he undertook to discharge. He over-rated his strength: he found the load too heavy to be borne. This is the simple truth. Silva was too sensitive to endure contact with the accumulated responsibilities heaped on him by the harsh fates. But his sensibility, too extreme for the crudeness of material existence, was the salvation of him as an artist. As a Colombian, he had a far wider knowledge of, and interest in, foreign literatures than is usual in Spain; his intellectual curiosity never slumbered; his fastidious ear found a heavy quality in what the Spaniards considered to be verbal music. He sought to substitute for these clangorous notes a melody more graduated, more elfin, more subtle. While still a very young man he began to publish in local papers poems which were recopied in the press of the Spanish-speaking world, poems that finally reached Spain by devious ways and struck the imagination of a few curious artificers. Silva's aims are set out in the poem which begins: '*Soñaba en ese entonces en forjar un poema* . . .' and which may also serve as an example of his manner. A sufficiently competent, though somewhat abbreviated, rendering (8) of these lines appeared in *The Westminster Gazette* of June 1, 1909, due, so I understand, to a man with a foreign name who has since perished in the plains of Picardy.

I swore I would write a poem, wrought
    from the dream of a dream,
Glowing, passionate, nervous, strong, audacious, supreme.

The rhythms floated before me, the rhythmical weaving of words,
Some like the shock of weapons, some like the song of birds,

Golden, and crowned in purple, the Sonnet stood forth as King,
But I chose me a simpler measure with bells and their echoing.

I chose it and decked it proudly, as one who would deck a bride,
With richest of rhymes of crystal, with rhymes of silver beside.

All of a sad, sad story, wherefrom the glamour had fled,
A tale of truth and a woman, beautiful, worshipped . . . dead.

Bitter; and so that I should not a shade of its bitterness miss,
I wrote it in words of the sweetest, soft as the touch of a kiss.

With gold I embroidered the phrases, and then to the syllables mute,
I wedded the mandoline's music, the faraway voice of the lute.

I shrouded the distance in vagueness, I filled in the foreground with light,
A Carnival's dazzle of brightness hurled glowingly into the night.

The mystic, the subtle, the sought-for I
    wrapped in the fleece of a veil,
The velvet of human temptations that faintly
    and vaguely assail.

Proud of my purple verses, born of the
    sunshine and mist,
I gave them the odour of lilac, the colour
    of amethyst.

I showed my dream to a critic, a critic
    stupendous, bland,
He read through it six times over—and said,
    'I don't understand'.

It depends, no doubt, on what the critic was looking for. He may have been a cousin of the mythical Senior Wrangler who remarked after reading *Paradise Lost*: 'It is all very well, but what does it prove?' Silva's critic must have been 'stupendous', indeed, if he did not perceive that he was dealing with something new in Spanish literature: a fresh appreciation of verbal values, a recognition of shades or *nuances*, a novel suppleness lent to a petrified metrical system. The 'stupendous' critic was less perspicacious than many readers of less pretensions to authority. It became the fashion to say that Silva had invented a new form of Castilian metrics. But it is not easy to invent a new form in metrics. And Silva himself was careful to disclaim anything of the sort. He pointed out that his innovation consisted chiefly in varying the stresses authorized by tradition, and took a certain malicious pleasure in asserting that he had found a model in Tomas de Iriarte, a prosaic intelligence but a virtuoso in the technicalities of verse.

Silva is a most interesting example of the cultured precursor, but he did not reside in Spain (I am not even sure that he visited that country when he was in Europe), and, as his poems were not collected till after his death, his influence in Spain, though very real, was necessarily limited in extent. The case was different in Spanish-America where his poems went the round of the Continent. They assuredly came under the eyes of a young man from Nicaragua, a man of about Silva's own age. I mean Rubén Darío who was born in 1867 and who died in 1916. A precocious lad, Darío began writing verses at a very early age, took to diplomacy, and was thus enabled to see much of the world. The chances of politics made him Minister of Nicaragua at Madrid in 1892, and he used his position as a ποῦ στῶ, and by precept and example imposed his poetic theories on the younger generation. You can tell instantly whether any given Spanish poet has lived after Darío or not. Perhaps nobody, since Boscan, has worked so complete a revolution in poetic methods. His earliest verses—those in *Epístolas y Poemas* (1885) and *Abrojos* (1887)—conform to Spanish tradition. Zorrilla, Campoamor, Núñez de Arce, and Bécquer have obviously been studied with extreme care. These works attracted no great attention in Spain. But in 1888 he issued a volume entitled *Azul* which came into the hands of Juan Valera. Now,

Valera, who declined to accept the popular verdict against his own verse, maintained his interest in poetry, and hailed *Azul* with enthusiastic praise. He allowed it to be seen, however, that he was disquieted at certain revolutionary symptoms discernible in the book. These he accounted for as being due to the bad example of the French on whom he launched the customary, conventional attack. But Darío paid no heed to the critic's warning; his manner became more and more pronounced in the sense that Valera disapproved, and finally Valera, who had no taste for swimming against the current of opinion, relapsed into a rather sulky silence. What, it may be asked, is Darío's chief distinction? His achievement in the field of prosody. His predecessors had practically confined themselves to the hendecasyllabic, octosyllabic, and heptasyllabic forms. Darío greatly increased the number of accepted metres in Spanish: introduced the enneasyllabic as well as the dodecasyllabic types, renewed the flexibility of both the old-fashioned Alexandrine (by changing the accent and altering the position of the caesura), resuscitated the hexameter which had been neglected since the time of Villegas in the seventeenth century, and finally was bold enough to transplant to Spain the *vers libre* (in which the number of feet, but not the foot itself, changes), as well as the type in which the number of syllables and feet vary frequently. He renewed the poetical vocabulary, banished the trite or worn phrase, and in fact succeeded where Góngora had failed. Withal, he remained a good Spanish-American, as well as a good European, a good Spaniard. He is representative of the two continents, and is hailed alike as a citizen of the Argentine Republic, and, as the statue in the Buen Retiro will show, a representative man of Spain. Though he died too soon for his friends, it was not too soon for poetry. His latest verses show unmistakable signs of fatigue. His work was done. Spanish poetry can never sink back into the old channels. Rubén Darío's influence lives and spreads in the verses of Villaespesa and especially in the admirable work of the younger Machado.

NOTES

(1) Longfellow's translation is now reproduced on p. 45 of the *Hispanic Anthology* collected and arranged by Thomas Walsh, Ph.D., Litt.D. (Hispanic Peninsular Series), New York, London, 1920.

(2) J. H. Wiffen, The Works of Garcilasso de la Vega, surnamed the Prince of Castilian Poets, translated into English Verse ; with a critical and historical essay on Spanish Poetry and a Life of the Author, London, 1823, p. 335.

(3) Idem, p. 348.

(4) *Hispanic Anthology*, New York, London, 1920, p. 171.

(5) *Hispanic Anthology*, New York, London, 1920, p. 248.

(6) *Obras poéticas de D. Luis de Góngora*, ed. R. Foulché-Delbosc. (Bibliotheca hispanica, xvi, xvii, xx), New York, 1921.

(7) E. Churton, *Gongora*. An Historical and Critical Essay on the Times of Philip III and IV of Spain, 2 vol., London, 1862 : vol. ii, p. 105.

(8) There exists a more literal rendering of Silva's poem by Dr. T. Walsh on p. 581 of the *Hispanic Anthology*.

INDEX

A
	PAGES
Acuña (Hernando de)	59
Alba (second Duke of) . 46, 52, 54, 55,	56
Alba (fifth Duke of) . . . 100,	103
Albornoz (Gil de)	15
Alburquerque (Duke of)	55
Alexandre (*Libro de*) . . . 8, 9,	10
Alfonso X, *el Sabio*	14
Alfonso XI [of Castile]	14
Alvarez de Villasandino (Alfonso) . .	32
Amadis de Gaula	82
Argote de Molina (Gonzalo) . . .	122
Ariosto (Lodovico) . . 104, 105, 106,	132
Avellaneda (Gertrudis de Gomez de Avellaneda y Arteaga)	170
'Azorín' (José Martinez Ruiz) . .	130

B
Baena (Juan Alfonso de)	30-1
Baralt (Rafael Maria)	170
Bataille de Karesme et de Charnage . .	17
Bécquer (Gustavo Adolfo) . . 163-4,	179
Bell (Aubrey F. G.)	31
Belleforest (François de)	72
Bello (Andrés)	170
Bembo (Pietro) . . . 48, 57,	63
Berceo (Gonzalo de) . . 3-14, 15, 16,	17
Black Prince (The) 3,	25
Boccaccio . . . 26, 27, 29, 36,	37
Borgia (St. Francis)	59
Borrow (George) 3, 105,	106

INDEX

	PAGES
Boscan Almogaver (Juan)	46-50, 52, 54, 60, 61, 63, 65, 66, 71, 72, 132, 150, 179.
Bouterwek Friedrich)	12, 13
Browning (Robert)	31
Burke (Edmund)	154
Byron (George Gordon Noel, Lord)	100, 157, 158, 167.

C

Calderon de la Barca Henao de la Barrera y Riaño (Pedro)	43, 82, 153, 154
Campoamor y Campoosorio (Ramon de)	159-62, 163, 172, 179.
Cancionero de Baena	30-1, 32, 34, 35, 36
Caro (Annibale)	57
Carpio (Bernardo del)	96
Carpio y Lujan (Lope Felix del)	101, 111, 112
Carrillo y Sotomayor (Luis)	136, 137, 151
Cascales (Francisco)	146
Castelar y Ripoll (Emilio)	120
Castillejo (Cristóbal de)	66
Castro y Murguia (Rosalia de)	171-2
Catholic Kings (The)	45
Celestina (*La*)	18, 33
Cervantes Saavedra (Miguel de)	16, 41, 43, 51, 59, 69, 79, 82, 94, 95, 98, 100, 102, 109, 113, 127, 133, 141, 148.
Cid (*Poema del*)	7, 8, 156
Claudian	97
Condé (Louis, Prince de)	153
Conn (George)	110
Corneille (Pierre)	43
Croce (Benedetto)	56
Cross (St. John of the)	65, 73, 74, 85, 86-93
Cueva (Isabel de la)	55

Ch.

	PAGES
Chacon Ponce de Leon (Antonio)	142
Charles V . 45, 52, 53, 54, 55, 57, 58,	155
Chartier (Alain)	38
Churton (Edward)	85, 147

D

Dante 29, 35, 37, 38, 40,	63
Dario (Rubén)	179-82
Debussy (Claude Achille)	164
Drake (Sir Francis)	101, 102.
Drummond of Hawthornden (William)	72
Du Bartas (Guillaume de Saluste)	71

E

Escrivá (El Comendador Joan)	82
Espinosa (Pedro)	128, 133
Espronceda y Lara (José Ignacio Xavier Oriol Encarnacion de)	157-8, 170
Estébanez Calderon (Serafin)	91, 92

F

Fe (Fernando)	159
Fernandez de Moratin (Nicolas Martin)	154
Fernando IV [of Castile]	14
Fernando VII	155
Ferrari (Emilio)	169
Floire et Blanceflor	9
Floranes Velez de Robles y Encinas (Rafael de)	10
Foulché-Delbosc (Raymond)	141
Francis I 53, 54,	57
Fraunce (Abraham)	71
Frere (John Hookham)	13, 156
Froude (James Anthony)	79

INDEX

G
	PAGES
Gallego (Juan Nicasio)	155
Gautier de Châtillon	9
Gomez de Avellaneda y Arteaga (Gertrudis)	170
Gomez de Quevedo y Villegas, Francisco	30, 83, 91, 92, 95
Góngora (Luis de)	60, 103, 119-52, 181
Gonzalez (Diego Tadeo)	154
Gracian y Morales (Baltasar)	83
Granson (Othon de)	38
Gregory (Saint)	26
Guardo (Juana de)	103, 104
Gutiérrez González (Gregorio)	170
Guzman (Fray Domingo de)	51
Guzman (Fernando de)	51

H
Hartzenbusch (Juan Eugenio)	30
Heine (Heinrich)	163
Henry II [of Castile]	24, 26
Henry III [of Castile]	26, 27
Henry IV [of Castile]	33, 44
Heredia (José-Maria de), *the French poet*	139
Heredia (José María de), *the Cuban poet*	170
Herrera (Fernando de)	49, 132, 133, 134
Homer	144
Horace	63
Hugo (Victor)	172
Hurtado de Mendoza (Diego)	36

I
Imperial (Francisco)	35-6, 48
Iriarte y Oropesa (Tomas de)	178
Isabel [of Portugal], *wife of John II*	33
Isabel [of Portugal], *wife of Charles V*	53, 55

AND MONOGRAPHS VII

	PAGES
Isabel II	165
Isabel de Jesús (Sor) . . .	. 83, 87
Isidore (Saint)	26, 104
Isidore (Saint, *of Madrid*) . . .	104

J

John I [of Castile]	. 25, 26
John II [of Castile] 27, 28, 30, 33, 37,	40, 44
Jonson (Ben)	120
Josephus	9
Jovellanos (Gaspar Melchor de) . .	154
Juana, *wife of Henry IV*	33
Juana Inés de la Cruz (Sor) . . .	169

K

Knapp (William Ireland). . . . 106

L

Lambert le Tors	9
Larra (Mariano José de) . . .	33
Lasso de la Vega (Garci) 47, 50–72, 73, 74, 89, 131, 132.	
Lasso de la Vega (Pedro) . .	52, 155
Lazarillo de Tormes (*La vida de*) . .	18
Lemos (Conde de)	100
Leon (Luis de)	. 65, 77
Lerma (Duke of)	129, 135
Liñan de Riaza (Pedro) . . .	145
Livy	26
Longfellow (Henry Wadsworth) . .	13
Lopez de Ayala (Pero) . . 4, 24–7,	29, 35
Lopez de Mendoza (Iñigo, Marqués de Santillana) 33, 36–9,	48, 66
Lopez de Vicuña (Juan)	143
Lopez de Villalobos (Francisco) . .	82

INDEX

	PAGES
Lujan (Micaela de)	101
Luther (Martin)	167
Lyly (John)	124

M

Macias, o *Namorado*	32-3
Machado (Antonio)	182
March (Auzias)	49
Mariana (Juan de)	109
Marino (Giovanni Battista)	135
Martial	63
Martinez de Medina (Gonzalo)	36
Martinez de la Rosa (Francisco de Paula Jerónimo Meliton Manuel Josef Maria del Carmen)	156
Martínez Ruiz (José)	130
Melendez Valdés (Juan)	154
Mena (Juan de)	39-42, 48
Menéndez y Pelayo (Marcelino)	13
Meung (Jean de)	38
Michaëlis de Vasconcellos (Señora Dª Carolina)	12
Milton (John)	43
Mira de Mescua (Antonio)	2
Molière (Jean Baptiste Poquelin de)	43
Molza (Francesco)	57
Moratin (Nicolas Martin Fernandez de)	154
Morris (William)	139

N

Napoléon Bonaparte	154, 155
Navagero (Andrea)	46, 47, 48, 49
Navarro Tomás (Tomás)	62
Nevares Santoyo (Marta de)	109, 110, 112
Núñez de Arce (Gaspar Esteban)	67, 164-9, 179

AND MONOGRAPHS — VII

INDEX

O
	PAGES
Olivares (Conde-Duque de)	142
Olmedo (José Joaquín de)	170
Osorio (Elena)	98, 99

P
Paez de Ribera (Ruy)	36
Pamphilus de Amore	17
Pardo (Felipe)	170
Pedro (Don), Constable of Portugal	38
Pellicer de Salas y Tovar (José)	146
Perez de Montalban (Juan)	95
Peter *the Cruel*	24, 25, 26, 27
Petrarch	37, 63, 70, 110, 132
Philip III	129
Philip IV	130

Q
| Quevedo (Francisco Gomez de) | 30, 83, 91, 92, 95 |
| Quintana (Manuel Josef) | 155 |

R
Racine (Jean)	43
Regnier (Mathurin)	18
Reina (Manuel Francisco de Asís)	169
Rivas (Duque de)	156-7
Rodriguez (Gonçalo), *Archdeacon of Toro*	31-2
Rodriguez de la Cámara (o del Padron, Juan)	32, 33-4
Rojas Zorrilla (Francisco de)	30
Ronsard (Pierre de)	67, 68, 69
Ros de Olano (Antonio)	152
Rossetti (Dante Gabriel)	139
Ruiz (Juan), *Archpriest of Hita*	15-24, 26, 38, 44
Ruiz de Alarcon y Mendoza (Juan)	30
Ruiz de la Vega (Gonzalo)	51

INDEX

S

	PAGES
Saintsbury (George)	62, 63
Sanchez (Francisco), *el Brocense*	62, 72
Sanchez (Tomas Antonio)	11
Sancho IV [of Castile]	14
Sanín Cano (Baldomero)	173
Sannazaro (Jacopo)	60, 63
Santillana (Marqués de)	33, 36-9, 48, 66
Seneca	120, 121
Shakespeare (William)	43, 167
Silva (José Asunción)	173-8
Sisebut	120
Statius	9
Stúñiga (Elena)	53
Swinburne (Algernon Charles)	139
Symons (Arthur)	89

T

Tansillo (Luigi)	57, 63
Telesio (Antonio)	57
Tennyson (Alfred, Lord)	62, 139, 167
Teresa de Jesús (Santa)	73, 74-86, 87, 88, 89, 92
Ticknor (George)	149
'Tirso de Molina'	122

U

Urbina (Isabel de)	99
Urrea (Jerónimo Ximenez de)	59

V

Valdés (Juan)	57
Valencia (Pedro de)	138
Valera y Alcalá Galiano (Juan)	152, 179, 180
Vega (Ventura de la)	170

AND MONOGRAPHS   VII

INDEX

PAGES

Vega Carpio (Lope Felix de)   41, 43, 94–118, 119, 133, 139, 140, 141, 145, 148, 149, 153.
Vega y Mendoza (Francisco de la) . . 51
Velazquez (Diego Rodriguez de Silva y) . 131
Velazquez (Jerónimo) 98
Verlaine (Paul) 80
Verstegan (Richard) 118
Vigny (Alfred de) 123
Villaespesa (Francisco) 182
Villafranca (Marqués de) 56
Villegas (Esteban Manuel de) . . . 181
Villena (Enrique de) . 28–30, 32, 35, 37, 39
Villena (Marqués de) [Juan Manuel Fernandez Pacheco, marqués de Villena y duque de Escalona] 28
Virgil 29, 37, 63

W

Wiffen (Jeremiah Holmes) . . 61

X

Ximenez de Urrea (Jerónimo) . . . 59
Ximenez Paton (Bartolomé) . . 134

Z

Zorrilla y Moral (José) . . 158–9, 179

HISPANIC NOTES

28895